Yoann MERITZA

GUARANTEED
SUCCESS

TAKE BACK CONTROL OF YOUR
DESTINY

Editor :
BoD-Books on Demand,
12/14 rond point des Champs Élysées
75008 Paris, France

Printing : BoD-Books on Demand, Norderstedt,
Allemagne

Legal deposit November 2018
ISBN : 9782322089949

Cover photo :
License : cco 1.0 universal / (cco 1.0)
Graphic design : :
Author: Yoann MERITZA

"The most worthy use of happiness is to use it for the use of others."

(Marivaux "l'Ile de la raison" 1727, act III, scene 9)

A FEW WORDS ABOUT THE AUTHOR

Yoann MERITZA is an essayist with a passion for personal development and human behavior.

Born on 28 March 1978 in Bonneville, Haute-Savoie, into a working family, he nevertheless benefited from schooling in private Catholic institutions, in particular in Sainte Bernadette and Saint Jean Bosco en Cluses, in his birth department.

His father, Constant Georges, who died on July 5, 2011 at the age of 81, a veteran of Indochina war, former member of the TOE-GCI, a civilian truck driver, suffered from throat cancer in 1981, always fought and cultivated enthusiasm despite his disability, because he understood how precious life was and that life had to be lived intensely. He was a veteran both during the Indochina war, and fought for the rest of his life.

Yoann was immersed in this environment where you had to fight every day, always trying to move forward no matter what and trying new experiences.

He followed a normal schooling until 1993 before going to an apprenticeship school in Saint Jeoire where he discovered the trades of electrician, carpenter, bar turner and welder, which made him a "versatile worker".

In September 1995, a new turning point in his life, he followed a trajectory in the tertiary sector of accounting at the Lycée Professionnel Privé "les cordeliers" de Cluses, where he discovered office automation and administration, and also learned information technologies for management, which he still uses today in his private life. But he missed his BEP by a few points.

Under the direction of his former accounting professor, he repeated his BEP in 1998, which he obtained.

From February 1999 to December of the same year, he performed his national service in Auxonne in Burgundy in the 511th Regiment of the train, then in the 27th BCA in Cran-Gevrier in Haute-Savoie.

After leaving the army, he decided to try his baccalaureate in accounting as a free candidate, worked for months in all subjects, became his "own teacher", even today, self-taught to the core, he knew how to "train himself", graduated, but decided not to stop, feeling like wings growing behind him, worked in the industry to finance his studies by correspondence in accountancy, which was "a big part" for him, every night taking his classes, but the results were scarce for him.

He undertook to resume his studies in recurrent session in 2001, make request of the training centers and the "Information and Orientation Center" (CIO), where he was followed by a counselor who helped him fill in the forms necessary for his reintegration into the professional cycle.

In September 2001, he studied at the Lycée Guillaume Fichet, he was then 23 years old, four of which separated him from the other students younger people, a slight generational shock which he managed to compensate, he adapted very well to this environment, and in June 2003 he obtained his professional laureate in accounting.

He tried hard to pass his BTS, because at 25 he was too old for employers when it came to immersing himself in a professional environment in two years. He suffered defeats, but always returned to the stage. He participated in some seminars for major car brands, especially in Valence, in the Drôme department.

In 2004, he took a golden opportunity and followed a training as a PME/PMI collaborator at the Chamber of Commerce and Industry at Scionzier in Haute-Savoie, where he discovered NLP (Neurolinguistic Programming) where he learned the tools to shape the subconscious mind and to manage human nature.

Since 2007 until now, he has been interested in the topics of personal development, subconscious control and has read many books on topics of psychology and behavior, he has also attended coaching seminars. He still follows the personal development coaches quite regularly.

He is also a member of the National Union of Combatants (UNC-Alpes), and the 27th BCA.

FOREWORD

*"Everyone knew it was impossible to do.
Then one day someone came who didn't
know, and he did.
(Winston Churchill)*

Hello everyone, you who are reading these lines,

The purpose of this book is to provide you with all the help you need to improve your daily life that will lead you, if you really want to, to success . It will fill in the gaps in your mind regarding the field of attraction.

For to be honest from the beginning, you will have many tools that I will provide you through the pages, but you will have to involve yourself personally. I'm not a magician or a dream salesman, I'm just highlighting what's already in you, that is, your ability to be better and move forward. If you want to give me a role, it will be like guide.

From very early in my life, I became interested in personal development, starting with a book by Norman Vincent Peal "the power of positive thinking", I was so fascinated that I read another, then another, and so on, I didn't even think of writing my own book one day, feeling unable to do so, but finally, and thanks to "my coaches" (alive or dead), and the "secret" (I'll come back to it), I had the courage and the strength to act.

I've gone through the whole question several times, it was exactly like you a short time ago, and I said to myself, "if my strategy doesn't work, you have to try another one", the problem, I was turning it upside down, and there are very few books that try in depth to be able to probe your own mind, because in my knowledge, the subject is vast.

It took me a lot of informations and reading before to publish this book, authors in personal development such as Max Piccinini, Mickaël Losier, Franck Nicolas, Napoléon Hill (as I affectionately call him my thought master), Florence Shoven Shyn, Emile Coué and Norman Vincent Peal. They are all what I consider friends from the heart, I owe them a lot, they have all helped me to open the way to the best of myself, and as they have done, I am transmitting knowledge to you in the field, I will help them answer the questions that are asked on the subject. Why doesn't it work like we would?

What is it that's blocking inside you?

All writers in the field of constructive thinking, as they are, are right, there are reasons why nothing works the way you would like and it comes from yourself.

If some people do the best they can and nothing succeeds, it is because, unconsciously, they have not done things the way they should. The essential was missing.

In this book, I will reveal something fabulous that can change your life forever, a power we all have, to overcome social barriers, to be a better version of yourself, what I very precisely call "The Secret".

The day I discovered "The Secret" was a revelation to me, my life took a big step forward, in what circumstances did I discover it? To explain it all, it was on New Year's Eve 2017, at the Chamonix Casino, a well-dressed old lady of well-to-do appearance, the "chic touch" as I might call it, told me a fabulous story, the one that made her triumph.

After the twelve midnight hits, we were talking about things and others, with a glass of champagne at the hand. The guests began to go home, the big room upstairs was emptying, there were only a few people left, including me, my current partner and this unknown woman.

We talked about our lives, about our trip in turn, and then she felt a little more confident, I remember she grabbed my arm and said "it's time to change direction, young man! "talking about my professional life.

She took out a kind of notebook with a pen and wrote something on it, then tore up a piece of paper with his notes. She folded it into four and gave it to me, saying, "When the day comes, you'll need it," then I put it in my jacket pocket.

I have kept these notes that contain "The Secret" as a precious good, what was noted above will impact you and will be revealed to you through the pages, because there are steps to follow, this power is very powerful, it is in each one of us, he can to built as it can to destroy according to how we use it, it requires a certain state of mind at a given time, do not worry, I will show you how to use it.

The following year, I did not see it again, but these words of our conversation were engraved

in my mind, "the positive attracts the positive".
». Remember of this you too!

Many people spend their lives ignoring that power, that of attractiveness, to get everything we want in our lives, to be recognized, rich in knowledge, to be able to afford a vacation, to go wherever we want. When I discovered this, everything seemed clearer in my mind, I was on the wrong track. Imagine you have this in your hands, this secret formula.

Many people go through life without trying the experience, they come to the end of their lives to say to themselves "if I had known! "Do you want to live with remorse, or change radically? Of course? I propose the definitive solution, the one that no one who knows it will tell you, because it is really very powerful, "but" (because there is a "but") this power has a darker side, it is the most terrifying aspect, and I will avoid this trap for you. All the "Secret" will be to you revealed. But it works, I can guarantee it works!

As mentioned earlier, this book is not a magic book, but it has the power to make your subconscious react, which can turn your dreams into reality. There is a fabulous power, the power to control your thoughts and make them come true, have a big house, have a nice car, get a good job, and everything you dream of, everything is within your reach here and now in these pages.

We can attract to ourselves everything we want, according to the law of attraction. Attention! There are conditions for this to act on you, materialization does not work if your thoughts are accompanied by a feeling of absolute necessity, it is essential to think that everything is already within your reach, it requires constant concentration and hide the brakes of your desires, forget your ego.

The chapters have been designed in a well-defined order, as they include steps for progress. If you are not a regular reader, or if you have very little time to devote, I recommend that you use a marker. You can read one chapter at a time, or about twenty pages, it's up to you.

I will go deeper, try to get to the source of yourself, exploit your abilities and finally break this shell, cut the Gordian knot of your existence. You explain how someone who is obviously not involved in anything suddenly made a new beginning. Like you, my life has been a succession of trials and failures, I will show you that with infallible will and determination, we can accomplish anything.

As you read, you will develop a taste for it, you will become a knowledge junkie, and you will know a little more than the day before. Through simple techniques, I will teach you how to become an improved version of yourself.

Don't rush the steps! Start this book in silence from the beginning, it is useless to go on to the following chapters without understanding the substance of the previous ones, it would be like watching a video in the last few minutes without understanding the substance of the story, or why it started.

The methods in this book work, and besides, they are free (well almost), I don't sell you the dream but I only take out what you have in you by the power of your thoughts, they can build like they can destroy your life, depending on how you use that power.

You will find, within this book:

- *Theoretical analysis,* summarizing in detail the transmission of the knowledge received in the field. The secret will be revealed to you gradually.

- *Practical tips,* to have the right habits to develop, to gain more self-confidence and to unleash the phenomenon of attraction in you.

- *Anecdotes*, wanting to share a little of my background and forge a bond between you and me, from confidant to confidant, and known and unknown personalities.

I will teach you to "do" and "believe," and to decipher the origins of your mistaken beliefs, which you have been taught. Break the cement that has been placed around you that prevents you from moving and advancing. Do you want the best of yourself? This should involve, first of all, a personal analysis, approaching the circumstances that describe why you are here, in this situation.

Together with you, I will develop along the pages a program to replace negative thinking and transform it into positive thinking. I invite you to apply, immediately after reading, the methods I propose in this book.

Don't be the victim of your life anymore, act now and believe in yourself! Value does not wait for the number of years, it is never too late. Control yourself by controlling your destiny. It is not by turning towards the end of your life that you will say "if I had known! »

Success is not a question of social environment, let alone luck (at least, the interpretation we make of it). Anyone who can afford it can do it, if they really believe in it.

I wish you all a good read, which I sincerely hope will become the gateway to your success.

Greetings;
Yoann MERITZA

INTRODUCTION

"Life is like a box of chocolates: you never know what you're going to find. »
(Tom Hanks / Forest Gump)

Our world is made up of almost 7,000 million people as I write these lines, because it is still a variable fact, a ceaseless tingling of men and women, there are births and deaths, a multitude of emotions generated every second, and somewhere in the midst of all this confusion, there is one person in particular, eyes open in this environment and full of emotions, this being who lives in the middle of this mess, you are the one who has my book in your hands, anxious to change the horizon of your life.

Why doesn't the law of attraction work for you? The question remains open to you despite all the efforts made to reach it. You have made desperate attempts, but nothing is happening.

Does it really work?

Yes, I clearly answer yes, but perhaps you are one of those who has already tried everything, all the existing methods on the subject, you have read books on personal development.

After following all the advice, nothing comes to you, it means that the problem comes from somewhere else, from the interpretation that is made of this power, from the negligence of seeing differently.

For example, if you have a car and it doesn't start, you have, among other possibilities, either to take it to the workshop or to try to find the fault on your own.

In the first case, you tell yourself that you don't know anything about it and take it to the workshop, with the risk of a costly intervention.

In a second case, it's about finding the fault, making dangerous assumptions about the reasons for the fault, part of the engine is removed, but you don't know how to reassemble it, there are many parts that lie on the ground. Overconfidence, combined with ignorance, will result in a more costly intervention than the first.

Third possibility, which is the right one and which will cost you nothing (only time and thought), you try to find the fault with a logical mind, you check oil, gasoline, in short, standard maintenance, battery condition, fuses, but you still can't find it. So you insist, look at the technical brochure in the glove box, consult on the Internet about similar problems and finally, "Eureka", has the solution, the diesel fuel supply wire was disconnected.

Sometimes we find it hard to find a complicated problem, wondering why your car does not start, when the solution is simple and within our reach.

I will show you in this book what is happening and that sometimes the solution seems easier than we thought.

His attempts can be summed up as trying to light a fire with a wet lighter in a torrential rain in Brittany (sorry for my Breton friends).

To answer them, and I will develop it in this book and for those who know the basic principles of personal development, it is not fate's fault and no one has bewitched you, you are not cursed by fate, I assure you, none of this.

To avoid being under the yoke of a "supposed" fatality, you must already get it out of your head. There is a way out that will help you progress, and it is useless to approach his mirror and wave his accusing little finger at you and say "it's your fault!

The problem is much more subtle, it is elsewhere, although part of your personality is against you, and it is related to your past, what you have experienced, the education and beliefs you have been taught, your need for social belonging in a world that has gone completely mad. To acquire a form of notoriety and recognition, but in what and in what quality?

As I said, everything that happens to you comes in large part from your beliefs and education, add your ego in addition, and you have all the ingredients that do not make you evolve, I ask you to be very careful with these last points.

You would like to go down in history, to be recognized, but for that to happen, you will have to be known that you are nobody for ordinary people, otherwise, you could also sell refrigerators in Greenland or radiators in the confines of the Sahara desert, in other words, it is useless.

Your existence will depend on the interest you show in others, because they are a reflection of your soul, of your being, and if you know the laws of causality, you attract to yourself what you give in others.

The man or woman is his own mirror. When you have people who know you and whom you have ignored, do not be surprised to be ignored at the same time, if you could see your behavior with their eyes, you would say "Oh my God, what an ungrateful person! "or "what a selfish man! "In short, she is badly compromised enough to give a good image. Unlike some people who have never tasted what you are before, there is always the possibility of giving them the best of yourself.

What needs to be changed first is your attitude towards others and yourself. Both our inner and outer world. We all have an energetic capital that is positively or negatively charged, and for those who know what I am talking about, after having studied the law of attraction.

We are all equipped with a vibratory bubble around us, inside, you perceive the outside world, the two are united, which you are, determines what the others are, the rule is universal. Don't judge others if you don't want to be judged negatively (human nature always judges no matter what happens), look at the world differently, and in turn, it will observe you differently.

If there is a change to be made, it will have to be made gradually for those you know, both friends and family, it may surprise them and make them wonder if you are taking drugs. The easiest thing is to start with simple words and gestures of complacency, to learn to say "hello", "goodbye", "thank you", etc....... it is the basis, it is education. So smile on the positive side, you are healthy, you have a roof over your head, how can you imagine getting more out of life if you are not already satisfied with what you have? You have everything to be happy, "Hight Tech" is really secondary, there are simple pleasures that life provides, don't neglect them!

Why nothing happen at you? Let's look at the problem the other way around:

In 1963, in Grant Pass, Oregon, a young athlete attended a high school meeting organized by the Rotary Club. He was fragile and unlikely to succeed and become the famous person he is today.

Indeed, having practiced high jumping since the age of 10, he never stopped finding a way to perfect his technique, as he could not reach the goal he had set for himself, which was to surpass two meters in height, and he jump only 1.80 m high.

Against all expectations, during the meeting, he managed to pass the two meters, making him different from the other competitors, instead of passing the bar over his stomach, he passed it over his back, to achieve this feat, he had to change his technique, since it was not working.

His jump, which was validated by the judges of the time, bears the name of the man who did the feat, it is called "the Fosbury".

If he did something impossible for him at the time, why shouldn't it be the same for you?

Maybe it's just a question of how to change the method, sometimes we tend to come across something conventional, without taking the problem any other way.

Hence the meaning of this book which is to see a different approach to what is already known, you have probably already tried everything but nothing succeeds, why? You have the knowledge on the subject of personal development and the law of attraction, written by very good authors whom I personally appreciate and who have trained you intensely.

They provide you with very good tools, it's up to you to use them! Seminars are not just opportunities to take pictures with them and post on Facebook, although it may seem like a good thing to do.

The problem don't come from them, they do an excellent job, so it can only come from you and your degree of investment in the subject, how to interpret the law of attraction and personal development for you?

The problem comes only from you, it is like a short-sighted person who looks in vain for his glasses sul the nose. For the law of attraction, it is the same, you look for the problem when it is simply inside you. Not all conditions are met to attract your desires to you.

We call it the "law of attraction", because there are rules to respect and how to interpret them. This is largely due to your personal investment, both in your way of thinking and in your way of acting, the two are combined.

The laws of attraction exist and must be put into osmosis with what constitutes your entire entity, both your feelings, your patience and your capacity for analysis. They need three elements to function:

An internal environment:

— **positive thoughts**, which consists of working on yourself to attract to you the things you want, not looking at the clouds, but the sun that hides just behind, not letting yourself be influenced by what your loved ones say, change your mood! We are all capable of great things, and I say all of us, you who are reading thcsc lincs, you have a great inner force that only needs to be expressed, if that is not the case, then why are you reading this page? What brought you here?

—**self-abandonment without external influence,** you must not constantly think about the positive result to obtain, you must act in the direction of your projects in the present moment, without postponing, if you want to attract to yourself everything you want, you must let the object of your desires come to you, it would be like pushing a swing door, while the energy of attraction pushes to your side too. When we think about it more, all our expectations come true, don't be impatient.

— **a personal contribution,** a physical contribution, the gift of self, you get nothing for nothing! It will not come only if the situation in which it finds itself does not lend itself to it. To want is one thing, but to act on it is another, you have to find a starting point, your moment T that makes you advance, of course, nothing will be done in a snap of your fingers, it would be too beautiful.

The three are inseparable, for example, when you think of going somewhere, you pack your bags, they will not be packed only by the power of your mind. A plant needs water and sunlight to thrive, if there is neither of these two elements, it dies.

Life is a mountain road, behind there are valleys, imagine carrying sandbags that represent your load, represent your fears, doubts and desires. Get rid of these bags, and the journey will be lighter.

This is all part of a more or less lengthy process depending on the person, either introverted or extroverted, so let's get started right away.

This process is called "Cyclic" because our decisions have cycles (or revolutions), I give you, in this book, the instructions to use this process.

In other words, some people have more ease than others, but the purpose of this book remains the same, success, you will feel a sense of pride at the end.

Where are you in your life? What are your successes or failures?

First, look at yourself about what you have and what you lack.

Have you made any mistakes in your life? Yes, but you can't think about it forever. How determined are you to make your life a success?

All therapies must require a good diagnosis, otherwise it is useless! You could also put a bandage on an open wound, "three aspirins and back in a month! "Do you really think everything can be cured like this? A house without a foundation makes no sense. What

I'm trying to explain to you is that you have to go to the source of evil to treat it better, a doctor doesn't give drugs blindly without an accurate diagnosis.

This is the first step in your transformation, to get to the heart of the subject that I want to develop with you.

Breaking the Ties with Your Condition

What will be mentioned in this book comes from experiences known throughout my life to get to this phrase on this page, I know well that not all have lived the same experience, but you will find similarities. I will show you how to break the bonds of your current condition and adopt a new way of thinking.

First I will teach you to be stronger psychologically, because you can, believe me! We all have power within us, including you, is beyond anything you can imagine.

It is important to follow the first steps of this book before beginning the in-depth work on yourself.

PART I : THEORETICAL POINT OF VIEW

CHAPTER 1: DIAGNOSING THE ORIGIN OF OUR ILLS

"The best way to fight evil is determined progress in good. »
(Lao Tseu)

Why does nothing work the way we want?

When attempts at success are useless waste, we must seek explanations. Talking about what works without talking about what doesn't work is like giving an answer without questions.

What happened in our lives? From birth, we are all identical, we are not contaminated by external elements, at least the first years, then, little by little, we discover our environment in which we grow, everything we see or hear shapes our lives according to how we interpret the situation in our subconscious that creates all feelings, fear, doubt, joy, sadness and courage.

We all have a history that has led us to this point, nothing has happened on our own, there are circumstances that have led us to be such or such a person in such or such a place, the social environment plays a role, I would not hide it.

The environment in which we operate influences our state of mind. Living in an unhealthy building with neighborhood problems goes against our positive thoughts, oppression is pervasive, creating feelings of fear and stress on a daily basis.

You will understand that bathing in such an environment is not beneficial to our mood. You absorb it like a sponge.

This may not be the case for you, but if I am writing this book, it is to involve everyone, both those who do not live in the environment I describe. I say to myself, "Good for you! "and, on the other hand, it allows you to understand the people around you who are living in this situation.

Why do some individuals succeed in their life and others don't? I will try to answer that question as best I can.

First, there is the environment in which we were born and in which we evolved. This information seems to be frustrated by the interpretation we have made of this environment since childhood, either by will or by resignation, instilling more or less erroneous beliefs, the education of parents plays a role, the archetype of a father who spoils too much, or of a mother who is too protective, we are taught the prohibitions and what we must do according to them, our free will seems to be disturbed by being very young, this period in which our brain registers most of the information.

You are an integral part of a system called "the paradigm," a social code related to a group of individuals in your environment. If you were born into the working world, you unconsciously reproduced everything you saw or heard. You have learned to place yourself in a hierarchy, to hate business leaders or all those who succeed, when you want to become one of these people, there is a form of incompatibility in the will, it paralyzes you, it would be like saying "you want to be a boss, but you don't like it, so you won't like your futur yourself". "is anchored in you.

To describe the paradigm, let me give you an example:

An experiment was carried out with four monkeys in a zoo, in the center of the cage where they were standing, there is a ladder, above it, bananas.

One of the primates was climbing up the ladder to collect the bananas, and the other three were taking cold showers.

Then the one who climbed the ladder was removed and replaced by another, ignoring what had happened before. He is sitting in front of the ladder, and as soon as he put his foot on the first step, the other three monkeys began to growl (without a shower of cold water).

One of the primates, one of which had not yet climbed the ladder, was being replaced and then placed in front of the first step. Naturally, he began to ascend.

The last two monkeys, as well as the one who was not aware of the cold water jet, began to grunt.

Finally, those who at the beginning of the experiment had experienced the cold water jet are replaced by two others, none of them knew what would happen if they touched the bananas.

One of the new ones would start climbing the ladder, and the others would growl. They didn't know why, but it's always been that way.

I will have my own experience with you (no ladder, no bananas):

Take four pens, one green, one red, one blue and one black.

Write *"red" in "blue", "blue" in "green", "green" in "black" and "black" in "red"!*

Now, read as quickly as possible the colors you have written down (for now it's easy)

Then do the same, but just name the colors of the words (ah! seems to be slightly stuck!)

Then alternate, a word, a color (it becomes difficult)

To show you the impact the subconscious mind can have on how you interpret things, the paradigm is engraved in your subconscious mind, but with training, we can overcome this, nothing is impossible until we try.

Your mind has become a "golden idol" in your life, they are your deep convictions, you think you are sure you are right (your experiences have shaped you). You have your own beliefs without this being the absolute truth, they constitute a barrier to your success, it is your unconscious brakes that whisper to you "it is useless", "I have already tried", "it is not for me".

You lie to yourself by putting a protective bubble around you, it has something to do with your past, you avoid the fear of the mockery or of "what will we say about it", the fear of popular laughings blocks you at the point where you find yourself, in front of you, there is a barrier that seems insurmountable to you. Am I right or at least in part?

Don't forge a "golden idol" for yourself, don't act according to the beliefs of others and trust yourself and what you think is right.

There's also our character, from introverted and calm to extroverted and angry (and vice versa), which is part of our genetic heritage.

A restless and angry child will tend to be suspicious of his parents and teachers, while a quiet child will tend to obey, even under discomfort, will not seek conflict, but as the years go by, with the company he has known in positive or negative, his temperament will change to one side or the other. He could also rebel if he has the guts to do so.

Our soul acts like a sponge that absorbs all the positive and negative energies, what we feel, what we hear affects our moods and beliefs depending on the environment in which we live.

How to use your subconscious mind

Suppose you have to build a small stone house, you take blocks big enough to build it, you're sure of what you're doing and you think it's solid.

This little house is your pride, you have done it with your own hands and for years it has stood the test of time.

One day, a visiting architect saw your work and went to meet you this way: *"Is this your job?"*

Proudly, you replied, "*Yes, it is me!*"

He replied: "*I wonder how something so unstable to endure, in 10 years of experience, I've never seen anything like it! The stones are badly distributed, you're lucky I didn't fall on you.* "

This architect has sown the seed of doubt in you, and he will grow with your new convictions. Everything you were proud of has disappeared, this doubt grows and turns into fear, you check the structure of your house several times, you go round and round each time to look for possible defects, and at night, you have trouble closing your eyes.

You think about it all the time and say to yourself: "I hope it doesn't fall on me! »

In a very short time, this thought fades away, you tell yourself that there is no longer any reason to worry, that you worry about nothing, while you sleep in silence, what you thought was happening, in the middle of the night, "badaboom", it's a disaster.

What happened? Your convictions have been turned upside down. The stones represent your beliefs and the architect symbolizes judgments and criticisms. You check the walls and nothing happens, until the day you no longer do it (principle of the eleventh hour, I'll talk about this later!).

What I mean by this is that if you believe firmly in what you are building, it will last a long time, but if you let yourself be overwhelmed by criticism, everything falls apart, don't let yourself be carried away by judgments or criticisms, it's all about you and your beliefs. Your house, you can rebuild it better, learn from criticism, don't give up on what you hear or read in other places, and surpass yourself "whenever you want, you can". »

In our lives, we all have a treasure map, it's up to us to find it! You have something in you that is stronger than adversity, attracts from within and you no longer fear anything, move forward without fear!

It is never too late to change your life, to take another path, but above all, there is a great work of reconstruction, starting with the foundations.

The print and the matrix

We are all identical in origin, from the moment we are born, we have a carnal envelope that welcomes our spirit, it is this body that allows us to evolve in the world in which we live and interact with others.

Although our minds are identical, their ways of evolving differ according to two criteria: the environment in which we grow up and the way in which data is treated according to personal and inculcated beliefs.

What determines why some people struggle to survive, and others remain placid and frightened, are the traces left in our subconscious, the beliefs we create from the learning of life, what our teachers or parents have told us, the notions of what is right or wrong, the interpretation that has been made of it, that is, being a child who rebels and resists parental authority, who wants to break the prohibitions, and the wise child who wants to be obedient, for fear of making mistakes and wanting to run straight.

In our childhood, we were flooded with prohibitions in our minds, things that had to be done or not, brakes were imposed on our minds saying "it is not for us", without having taken the time to discover or try it, enclosing our curiosity in a Pandora's box form. And if we break the lock now, what will we find out? What's hidden inside? All the opportunities lost in the depths of popular or family beliefs, creating the dogma of so-called true thought, but nothing is closed at all, but we don't want to force prohibitions.

Not all of us have had the opportunity to be born or live in an easy environment conducive to positivity, there are people who are satisfied with what they have against their will, not by choice, but resignation has prevailed over their desire to get out of this environment, it is not like you who have chosen to get out of it, to get there in life, we must also recognize that everyone is different, so not everyone works in the same way.

The acceptance of your situation is the worst evil that can exist, I am not saying that in a given moment those I am talking about did not want to get away with it, it is a combination of events that have pushed you to accept it very sadly, pushing us into daily habits without necessarily realizing it at the beginning.

When you look at the daily lives of some people and the environment in which they live, it doesn't help either. As we project ourselves into the heads of these people, we feel the paralyzing mental disorder, as we project ourselves into them, what would we see in them?

I know that fear can paralyze the will, and that despite the desires, there is a background of fear and resignation that prevails. That's why I begin this book on a negative note, because evil must be healed at the root if we want to give ourselves the opportunity to change our lives and improve them.

Theoretical energy analysis

They work by resonance, what we call "vibratory fields", our body emits waves according to your mood of the moment and your feelings.

Unconsciously, we always do the same things, we always make the same mistakes, don't you see that life repeats itself over and over again? Because you are trapped in a circle, also known as the "vicious circle" or "infernal spiral".

Have you seen the film "An Endless Day", in which the protagonist repeated the same things over and over again? He managed to manage at the end by learning from his mistakes every day, it will be the same for you.

Imagine a whirlwind spinning counterclockwise with a large size, and a smaller whirlwind, just above it, spinning clockwise, these two whirlwinds represent accumulations of negative and positive energies, one not spinning without the other.

As we change our habits, negative energy will be transferred to positive energy, there will be a suction phenomenon that will be included from one vortex to another, you will feel weak at first in your environment.

To give a more accurate picture of this process, these cycles, as I like to call them, work like the sprockets of a clock (to better symbolize the passage of time). The largest sprocket is the negative energies, in this case the smallest represents the positive energies.

Both have a cycle (or revolution), if we mark one of the teeth of these two sprockets in a single stroke, we would realize that the revolution would be longer than the other, adding the time that passes, proportionally to make the journey itself, for example, one would make a journey in a year and the other in a month.

If all the decisions we make, the words we say and the paths we follow were written in these two speeds, the actions would be equivalent, and that's why when we embark on a project, we give up after a short time. Because the conditions are not met.

In the current situation, your subconscious mind unhook the gears that continue to spin separately and at the same time. It is as if you kept your foot on the clutch of your car, as long as you keep the pedal pressed, that is, as long as you "keep control", the vehicle does not advance, gradually release the pressure on it, the vehicle will start to advance, and that is why you need to build positive thoughts, do good deeds, consolidate everything in your mind, be morally strong, and when the time comes, when you feel ready, release the pressure on the clutch, in other words, "let go! This will lead to the pinion of positively charged energies.

You are always in the infernal spiral, when you start a project, make sure first that it is not a fantasy of your mind that only reproduces what you have seen on television or what you have been told.

In simple rules, build your mind with good thoughts and do good deeds, focus mainly on that, mark the ground, don't get unnecessarily involved, knowing you're not ready to get everything you want when the time comes, let it go.

For the moment, you are still prey to a mass of negative energies that you must evacuate, I know many are impatient, but be ready to receive when all conditions are met.

However, we can reverse the trend, make the positive cycle greater than the negative, we must be aware that everything is possible with a little will. No one is condemned to fate.

Thought has an enormous power of attraction and you use it unconsciously!

Do not think of the sky and the great storm will occur, do not imagine the lightning!

Right now, you've been thinking about it, haven't you? That's because your mind doesn't know denial.

You do things in your life that violate prohibitions, unconsciously, you do! For example, when you see a "don't come in" or "attention fresh paint" sign, your curiosity will take hold of you, you will be tempted to come in why you can't do it, or to touch the paint to check that it is fresh.

You should avoid projecting yourself into the future, ruminating on "as long as" or "if only".

For example, if you think, "as long as a tile doesn't fall on my head," the problem is that you've thought about it, and it could hurt when you're less attentive.

The tile will fall anyway, but don't worry, it will only be temporary, behind this "although", something wonderful is hidden, you have to see beyond the mountain, behind the clouds and the storm, there is a beautiful blue sky. Abstain from thinking about future events, they are very uncertain, if only to expect something wonderful.

I would never say it is impossible, but you have to put your heart into it and radically change your way of thinking. Transforming his weaknesses into strengths, knowing how to carry everything he has within himself by telling himself that fortunately there were those situations that woke me up and made me realize that real change was needed.

To do this, we will have to force the security mechanisms of our subconscious mind, which exists in three forms:

• **The abandonment mechanism** that tells us not to go any further and that this desired situation is not for us, it is better not to start and be satisfied with what we have. In this abandonment mechanism, we can include the desire to have projects, launch plans on the comet, and then say to ourselves: "After all, it's not for me. This happens in what could be called "the eleventh hour" (the limit), you are so close to it that something inside you makes you doubt it, there is a feeling of renunciation that is triggered, it deflates you just a few meters (or even a few centimeters) from the goal.

• **The prevention mechanism** innate in each one of us, is precisely the one that alerts us if we approach the hand of a boiling pot, our subconscious prevails over the will, and tells us "stop, it is dangerous! This is what allows us to keep control of events, we do not let them go, when for example we drive, if we are not attentive, it is the accident, beforehand, you would have said to yourself "as long as I do not have an accident! "Only when we let go of the guard, we don't even think about it anymore, does it happen. Believe it or not, the law of attraction works that way, positively and negatively, but it must be embedded in the subconscious and your paradigm.

• **the upset will,** which can be summed up as wanting something without giving oneself the means to achieve it. Besides, we don't make tortillas without breaking eggs. The frustrated will is also characterized by an eternal struggle in your subconscious, you oscillate between two feelings and currents of thought, you want to triumph but on the other hand, those who triumph leave you a bitter taste, you want to be rich, but you despise the rich, you want to earn more money, but you feel that money does not make happiness, and this is part of your paradigm, you must learn to love all the things you want to achieve it in turn. Don't forget to be generous with life if you want she to be generous with you in return.

The notion of right and wrong in terms of energy

If we could transpose good or bad energetic influences into beliefs that are of the sacred order, we could get a view of what is right or wrong.

A little above, I mentioned the positive and negative energies in the form of whirlwinds, if we draw a line between the two, above would be heaven, and below hell.

We could very well talk about karma (or the boomerang effect), about the waves we make and send to the universe, which come back to us one day or another.

In symbolism, God represents virtue, the very traced path, the point at the top of the triangle of his head in a representation made of him, which has as a halo, indicates the direction of the elevation of consciousness, it also seems a path in perspective.

The Devil, on the other hand, represents vice, the tendency to drift, from curved paths like his horns, it's deviation.

The question is not whether I am right or wrong, but that you have complete freedom of conviction, just as I do.

God explains it differently in the seven capital sins and in the ten commandments, He gives us the way to virtue. It is a map, a plan of access to harmony and wisdom.

If you look closely, everything is consistent:

The greed determines not only the fact of eating, but also on a material level, is always wanting more and more without giving time or food. How can we expect to have more if we do not give to others? You will never (or rarely) be invited to a table if you do not invite yourself.

The laziness, There are people who don't bother to think, but who have all the skills to do it. There are people who were not lazy at the beginning of their lives, but who became lazy out of necessity, out of resignation, out of bad experiences in the past, because they got used to not trying anything else. Laziness, in a way, has returned as a culture of life.

The lust, greed, excessive carnal pleasures, such as greed, is always wanting more, a desire that is far from physical or spiritual love. Love and sex are inseparable, if there is no interest in the person you want to have sex with, your partner will lose interest in you, leaving you with a bad reputation as a flirt, male, speculator, etc.. Their image will be affected.

The desire to yield to temptation, to indulge, there is not necessarily any harm in that, as long as it does not impact others, it is also to show height without being up to the task. The desire to surpass without surpassing yourself.

The greed, who tends to be compulsively attached to material wealth, to the point of idolizing it. There is, in fact, a search for accumulation in order to acquire more and more, in an exaggerated and selfish way. Like greed or lust, it means wanting more, but keeping everything for yourself, it is not only about gold or jewels, but there is also on a material level, a bigger house, for example.

The anger attracts to you the harmful energies that destroy you spiritually, and sends unhealthy magnetic waves back to your surroundings. It is a disorderly movement of the mind toward violence, manifested by the bursting of voices (screams), vivid gestures, even offensive words and vengeance. The thoughts of revenge also have an impact, react very well to your current emotional state, is the osmosis between the two, your energies must be redirected to healthier thoughts.

The pride is the fact of attributing to oneself qualities that one does not have and returning everything to oneself, the proud person believes himself superior and more deserving than the other individuals he despises, we find these character traits in the narcissists.

These seven mortal sins have one thing in common, affect others, and return negative feelings, and what's more, they only concern your ego.

They are below the line and the whirlwind grows from these vices, giving it more force of attraction and any action taken to get out of it will be in vain if you do not change internally, you will have understood, the fact of relating everything to yourself, whether in any capital sin, will shut you up in this infernal spiral.

But after the clouds, let us talk a little about the sun! As I have already said, God shows us the way to follow.

He has set in motion clues in the form of theological virtues, they are not numerous, but if we believe in them, they will have the strength to get you out of the negative whirlwind.

In order to unleash in us the power of attraction of the positive energies, it is indispensable to follow a certain road map where the virtues that they are are:

The faith: It is to have confidence, to act without fear, to stay the course in all circumstances despite the obstacles of life, to have faith in your dreams, behind the obstacles there is always something wonderful, do not lose sight of your objectives. Keep this treasure within you, move forward no matter what, there will be pitfalls, but you will face the challenges with great success.

The hope: It can have two edges, nothing will come alone, you have to put your heart into it, there is no magic in vain in hope, you have to invest in the hope of succeeding without necessarily having everything the first time, never give up, hope and start over!

The charity: It is to forget oneself to dedicate oneself more to others, to give time or money, charity is to give positive energy to others, smiles and gratitude. Never forget that man is the reflection of your mirror, what you do for others, you do for yourself. Everything will inevitably come back to you if you are generous, you have the strength to forget yourself. When you throw a stick at a dog and he won't come looking for it for you, it's because if you look at your hand, you'll see that it's still on a leash. Let go!

The theological virtues are above the line, in the positive whirlwind that will lead you to success.

This is what also differentiates an open mind from a closed mind, the negative waves always turn towards your ego, while the positive ones turn towards altruism, think about it! What do you want to do today for others? What would be useful to them?

You release a harmful aura that is felt when you turn to yourself, this need for belonging and superiority makes you feel afraid around you, learning to look at the behavior of certain individuals in your presence, this says a lot about who you are.

Do not give existence to evil, it feeds on your beliefs, the only way to destroy it is by ignoring it, it is a human creation through the trials we are going through, without finding guilty parties, we lean on it, it is a weakness of the spirit that materializes.

There is no avenging God either, it is love, and all the trials along the way are only the fruit of chance, it depends on how we approach the problem, or we become actors in our existence, or victims, there are no punishments from heaven, you inflict it on yourself with your stagnation, your fears and beliefs, good and evil are in you, and it is you who feeds on your thoughts and actions.

If the universe is a "whole", you are part of that "whole", of what you see, feel, hear and touch, everything is connected. God is in all things of the universe, in the air we breathe, in the mountains we see, in the flowers that grow in the meadows, is the same for you, is the vital energy. Its opposite is the evil that destroys this vital energy, and depends on your contribution through cunning playing with your emotions, feeds on your fears, your anger and all other unhealthy feelings.

When you understand the importance of belonging to all things, of being part of them as an element, then be aware that you have this part of a "whole", and there is no limit, what you want, what you already have, because everything is linked.

To explain to you in more detail what evil is, it is what stands between your being and divine power.

Speaking of pictorial form, it is reduced to incompatibility, it is about inviting yourself to everything you think, drink or smell. If God is the creator of a "whole", the devil uses his work to divert it.

I encourage you to read Napoleon Hill's work "more intelligent than the devil", this book explains why men acquire the habit of deriving from their early years, their education and the interpretation of it.

The Karma

I am not asking everyone to adhere to all my beliefs, but if you are looking for a better life, spirituality can help you.

For those who believe in the laws of karma, all actions, good or bad, return to us with the same intensity, more or less long term.

To describe the principle to you, to see the people around you as your own reflection, if you steal from someone, it will happen to you one day or another, if you are disrespectful, you will not be respected, but if you are generous, people will be generous to you, it is a universal law.

The term "karma" in Sanskrit means "actions", each "action" leads to a reaction, and this has a connection with what we do in the moment or in the past that emerges at a more or less unexpected moment in our lives. Everything comes back to us at some point without us waiting for it, or unconsciously, we knew it would happen. For example, suppose you play squash, a second of inattention, and the ball comes back to us at whole face, so we have to be attentive to what we send into the universe, because there is what is called "the shock of return," or "the eleventh houre".

What we call "eleventh houre" are the circumstances that happen when we don't think about it at all, our attention is relaxed. The reason for this is that our subconscious mind blocks the flow of positive or negative energies, and when we let go of the object of our thoughts, everything ends up happening, just like when we play squash, if we let go of our guard, the ball can come directly on top of us, and it would be better if they were good events.

The karma, for the uninitiated, contains twelve laws to respect in order to maintain a healthy life:

1) The Great Law

"When you sow, you reap it. "This is also known as the "law of cause and effect. "Everything we emit in the Universe comes back to us. If what we want is happiness, peace, love, friendship, then we must be happy, peaceful, loving and a true friend.

2) The Law of Creation

Life not only happens, it needs our participation. We are one with the Universe, both within and without. Be yourself, and Surround yourself with what you want to have in your present life.

3) The law of humility

What you refuse to accept will continue to catch up. If what we see is an enemy, or someone who has a character trait that we consider negative, then we are not focusing on a higher standard of living.

4) The Law of Growth

"You're where you want to go. "Growing in spirit means that it is we who must change, not the people, places or things around us. The only thing we are given in life is ourselves, and it is the only factor over which we have control. We change the person we are in our heart, our life follows movement and changes.

5) The Liability Act

Every time there's something wrong with my life, there's something wrong with me. We are the mirror of what surrounds us, it is a universal truth. We must take responsibility for what is in our lives.

6) The Law of Connection

Even if something we do seems unimportant, it is very important that everything is done as everything that relates to the Universe. Each step, even the next, and so on. Someone has to do the initial work to give results. Neither the first nor the last step is of major importance, as both were necessary to carry out the task. The past, present and future are connected.

7) The Merger Law

You can't think of two things at the same time. When we focus on spiritual values, it is impossible for us to think of greed or anger.

8) The Law of Giving and Hospitality

If you believe that something is true, then in the course of your life, you will be called upon to demonstrate that particular truth. This is where we put into practice what we say we have learned.

9) The Law of Here and Now

Looking back to see what prevented us from being totally in the here and now. Old thoughts, old behavioral habits, old dreams prevent us from having new ones.

10) The Law of Change

History repeats itself until we learn the lessons we need to change our course.

11) The Law of Patience and Reward

All rewards require initial work. Sustainable rewards require patience and persistence. True joy continues to do what we are supposed to do, and waiting for the reward to come on its own.

12) The Law of Value and Inspiration

You get something back no matter what your contribution is. The true value of something is a direct consequence of the energy and intention you put into it. Each personal contribution also contributes to the whole. The lack of contribution has not been no impact on the whole and neither do they reduce it. Generous contributions bring life and infuse.

CHAPTER 2: WHAT'S BLOCKING YOU INSIDE?

Limitations and obstacles

Some of you probably have some obstacles to your projects: difficulties in concentrating and projecting, your thoughts remain blocked.

This is the phase of acceptance of fatality, a way of saying "what's the point?", "*it will never work*," *"I've already tried*,"... are you sure?

You are in a phase of limiting thoughts, a wall of false beliefs that has been built by people you have met in your life, instilling them in you.

Accepting who we are is the worst thing is fatalism, and reading some books on personal development will not be enough to address what is a fundamental problem, of course tools are provided, but the real work is up to you.

For the moment, you think you are safe in your comfort zone, your little house, your cat, your TV to watch "*Game of Thrones*" or another, the outside world does not reach you, it is an unconscious phenomenon of self-protection, everything is limited only to the bubble that forms around you, you look like a hamster on its wheel, to go around in circles, subway, work and sleep. Your life is that and nothing more, and you have to go beyond that, cross barriers that seem impassable to move forward, and regain control of your life instead of having it under control.

To discuss my point of view, let me tell you this story:

A man found an eagle egg one day and placed it in a pothole. The eagle was born in the middle of a litter of backyard chicks and grew like them. All its life the eagle did what a backyard hen normally does. It searched the ground for insects and food and was behaving in the same way as a backyard chicken. And when he was tempted to fly, he was in a cloud of feathers and only a few feet away.

After all, that's how backyard chickens are supposed to fly.

Years passed. And the eagle became very old. One day, he saw a beautiful bird gliding in a cloudless sky. Rising gracefully, he took advantage of the rising currents, barely moving his magnificent golden wings.

"What a splendid bird! "said our

eagle to his neighbors..." What's this?"

"It's an eagle, the king of the birds"..... he shouted to his neighbor..." But forget it. You'll never be an eagle. »

So the eagle never thought about it again.

He died thinking it was a backyard chicken.

So, I ask you the question, do you want to behave like a chicken or an eagle?

What is your true potential in life, have you ever used it?

The only obstacles that exist are those that you voluntarily or involuntarily impose on yourself.

Fear of reactions

We are at the heart of what gnaws at you, the impression you have towards people is that they have blinders, and do not necessarily admit the truth that you impose on them.

Of course, we can't guess everyone's state of mind, but their feelings and emotions remain the same.

You seem to be discreet at best, or indifferent at worst. In both situations, you have little or no interaction with others.

This blockage simply comes from you, how you want to be perceived (in your imagination) and how you perceive yourself. It is your ego that speaks, in all your actions, when you do something for others, you wonder how the action will be interpreted, good or bad, on the one hand you unconsciously seek recognition, and on the other hand you are afraid of criticism, both focus on yourself. It will be necessary to correct this behavior, to try to do gratuitous acts, without thinking about the esteem that we should give him! Your ego is the sign that you want to be superior, while unconsciously, you activate the laws of causality (or karma). Each individual is his own reflection, what you send to others is returned to you.

You are considering negative scenarios, such as people's irritability, misperception of self or mockery.

But the reality is that you remain in total ignorance, because you are not trying. You tell yourself that it is more comfortable not to say anything or do nothing, not to seek trouble with others, and at some point along the way, it is praiseworthy despite everything.

Imagine a line on the ground, representing what separates you from your goal.

Your reality is only one line, the interaction is limited, this line is called "ignorance", in the sense that on the other side of the line, you do not know how your fellow men will react, look around you, it is the same for each individual, and yet some have the audacity to cross this border represented by this line. On the other side is "knowledge", you know a little more about each other's intentions.

Of course, there are risks, there are disappointments too, but unlike others, because almost all are the same (except those who have crossed this line, like the great leaders), many are those who do not take the step into the unknown, and remain in stagnation with their "a-priori" about you and your companions.

So, unlike others who may criticize you, notwithstanding the situation in which they find themselves, that is, no more than you, mocking, irritating, impressing you, the step into real life will be taken, while others will stagnate, gnawing at their jealousy, full of remorse towards themselves, dressing you in many suits or nicknames.

In reality, it is up to you and them alone to succeed or not, and it is useless to criticize those who succeed, they have given themselves the means. To that, I'm going to ask you a question. Do you ever criticize rich and famous people? In front of your television, watching politicians or stars, you want to be in the place of these individuals, but you criticize these individuals.

If you become a future star or a politician (you never know!), would it seem normal for people to judge you? Those who do, will be exactly as you were!

Remember that man is the reflection of man, but that the two will not have the same point of view. One will hate the other and the other will wonder why he is hated, he is the present "you" and the future "you". Respect what you want to be!

If you hate those at the top of power, how do you want to do it if you send negative waves about what you want to become?

You're sending the wrong signal to the laws of attractiveness.

Part of the secret is there! Love what you want to be, imagine being in your shoes without judging your current actions, you don't know if you could do better as you don't know how your decisions will be perceived.

Don't let yourself be destabilized, go ahead and never stop.
If you don't believe what I'm telling you now, you should know that I was like you long before you started this long transformation of your mind, and look at yourself, before, I didn't know you, and now I'm both your confidant and friend in the sense that I'm acting like this, and what differentiates us, this line that separates us, pushes us to see that one holds the book and the other has written it, one is an actor, the other is spectator, you have proof that everything is possible and I invite you to join the ranks of the actors of the life.

What's stopping you from moving forward and making your dreams come true? In my own experience, renunciation or moving forward without a specific goal is limited by fear and lack, there are different types:

- Fear of failure: It's one of the obstacles that prevents you from advancing, you believe in your project and you want to succeed, it's commendable. However, you give up because of your "premonitory gifts", you guess beforehand that you will fail, so you don't try anything, which is a great pity. He refuses to face it or to be sure that he wants to be right, that he wants to protect his ideas, he thinks: "How can I get there without me failing?". You have to accept failures as opportunities to move on, not to keep your ideas frozen in time with questions, to know the why of how, if you fail, do it again! No victory is possible without disappointment, learn from your failures!

Several years ago, my brother and I were invited to a friend's house for coffee and to talk about things and other topics, we were in his apartment, and suddenly he started taking a game of chess on a shelf and put it on the table for us.

We were surprised by his attitude, and as he placed the pieces on the board, he asked us if we had already played. Very reluctant to show our ignorance, we replied that we had played this game before but it had been a long time ago.

So he explains the rules to us, and then asks us to start the game. Being a little embarrassed by our lack of knowledge, we passed our turn, and he moves his first piece.

What he said next made us think, here are his own words:

"Chess is life! »

What do you think he meant by that? In reality, you don't advance in life, whether you know the rules or not, because you are "stuck" and you don't try anything for fear of failure. So you pass your turn, and your opponent takes the risk for you, but he goes ahead.

You are so absorbed in your desire for victory that everything you do will succeed, with a "but if it fails..." "You don't know anything about it after all, the question remains open in time.

What if I told you that in order to succeed, you have to fail first? This would seem absurd to you, and yet everyone who has succeeded has experienced at least a first failure, nothing of what I know is done in the first attempt, failures should serve as a basis for learning, the more you fail, the more you learn, the stronger and more trained you become.

Write this on a white stone, on your desk, hanging from a wall, in great letters "to succeed, it's before to fail! ».

If you really want to move forward, go all the way of your project, even if it means screwing up, not living with great regrets without to know what's wrong, then start again!

Thomas Edison, when he invented the bulb, succeeded at the end of the 10,000th attempt to light it, and as he himself said, did not fail but found 9999 ways not to make it work.

- *fear of judgment:* Of course, you will not please everyone in your ideas, no matter what you do, you will be judged in good or evil, it is the nature of man.

One day, a boy asks his father a question:

- "Tell me, Dad, what's the secret to being happy?"

Knowing only to answer this question, the father suggested his son follow him. They left the house, the father on a old donkey and the next son on foot. The people of the village accused:

- His father is an unworthy father! He rides his donkey when his son follows him on foot!"

- Have you heard my son? Let's go home," said the father.

The next day they went out again, but this time the father put his son on the donkey and accompanied him, holding the bridle. The neighbors said:

- Here is an unworthy son! He rides his donkey when his father follows him on foot!"

- "Have you heard my son? Let's go home," said the father.

The next day, they both settled on the donkey and left the house. The villagers once again criticized the father and son:

- You don't respect your beast by overloading it like that! »

- "Have you heard my son? Let's go home. »

The next day, they left with their own things, the donkey trotting behind them. This time, the villagers found something more to say:

- "Now they carry their own luggage! It's the world upside down!"

- Have you heard my son? Let's go home. »

When they came home, the father told his son:

- The other day, you asked me about the secret of happiness. Whatever you do, there will always be someone to criticize you. »

DO WHAT YOU WANT AND YOU'LL BE HAPPY!

Fear of the procedure : It is to ask ourselves if we are doing the right thing or not, if we have not omitted anything, what steps to take and at what price, who to trust, if we will be paid and if we fail, will there be a problem?

— *Lack of resources :* you say to yourself, "What's the point of paying for an expensive education when it probably won't work? "Starting a business, whatever it is, always has a price to pay, it is discovered over time, you have to invest in capital goods and have enough capital to avoid the hassle of a blocked account or a letter from the bank. Of course, we'll have to save money (that's more than safe), we don't start in a business without a way to overcome the difficulties, and there will be some. Are you more like a cicada or an ant? The tendency is to spend money beyond our means to give us pleasure, it is not really a bad thing, but we must know the priorities and know what will be useful in the future, make good investments.

- *The lack of diplomas :* You want to start and you feel you don't have the diplomas or the knowledge to do it. I'm sorry to say it's a false excuse. Perhaps this was true a few decades ago, long before the advent of the Internet, but even without it, there are libraries, adult courses, counselling centres, and now it is possible to ask for advice and take action online. That is to say, also, for those who know the french singer Renaud, who started his career without any diploma in hand, look now where he is, he is part of this category of self-taught individuals (who have succeeded by themselves outside the school circuit).

- *Lack of perseverance:*It's your stubborn side of your personality that stands out, it's an unreasonable way to always go where the wind blows, to let go when you feel it's going to go wrong (well, what you say). Nothing is easy in life, if you want to succeed, you will have to invest in yourself. Never give up on the argument that you don't seem good enough, uninformed, afraid by judgement, or simply afraid to fail.

— *Lack of concentration :* It's hard for you to be calm, you're always interrupted for one reason or another, or you put your projects aside too much to find other distractions, moving a little further away from the initial goal.

Excesses

They can delay the realization of their dreams, there is an excess insurance, it is a source of many mistakes when it is misused. Never trust your routine insurance, it is often the trap, for example, make sure you close the door when you leave, we do it without even thinking about it, it is precisely the concern, we do not think about it!

If you know airline or recreational pilots, you should know that to land their aircraft, they must follow a procedure and be careful not to forget anything, in a commercial flight, the pilot listens to the instructions of the co-pilot who reads a list of maneuvers to perform: "*flaps? OK*", "*landing gear? OK*".

A tourist pilot should make the maneuvers alone, if he forgets the landing gear, probably distracted by the landscape or too sure of himself, "be carefull of damages!".

Excess ego and self-esteem : When confidence is too strong and you are convinced that you are right when you are constantly in error (*human nature! When you keep us!*), it is the temperament of the "*compulsive obstinate man*".

Lack of resources due to excesses

There are excesses linked to daily life, inseparable from the lack of everything, such as the desire to have a new PC, a new sofa, to be fashionable "touch" to please you, but that you don't have, after buying many different things, more money to insure your courses, is also a false excuse. Remember the fable of the cicada and the ant "the cicada that sang all summer was very private when winter arrived" (winter is the winter of your life, the last season).

Lack of information due to excessive laziness: or more clearly, the laziness of opening a book or getting information, sometimes you have to be violent with yourself, a little inner voice has to say "*Get up!* ". "Have discipline!"

The past

Sow the seeds of doubt, prohibition and fear that have grown in you. Disappointments, rejections, bad blows of life have slowed your existence.

Despite appearances, if you feel that your life has been a failure from the beginning, your past is part of you, when we use it well, it allows us to make the right decisions, the accumulated mistakes should make us realize that we have not made the right decisions and that we must start again. This is what gives you your identity, it is part of you, do not suddenly cut the umbilical cord between what has happened in your existence and the present moment.

You have to adopt a new way of thinking, a different philosophy of life, and learn to be grateful for all the challenges that make you stronger. Use it! Learn the lessons and today is an opportunity to start over on a new foundation, to improve your daily life and your relationships with others.

Don't let your past dominate you, and dominate your past!

Where's the "limit"?

We discover this limit when our emotional state changes, going through fear, enthusiasm or doubt, for example, if you plan to bungee jump, it is when you are above the void, ready to throw yourself that you discover the "limit" of your subconscious, alert all your senses, put a barrier in front of you and prevent you from falling forward, but once you are hung in the void, something powerful fires in you that takes your breath away, is "the little death", our existence becomes superfluous, the road crosses. Many of the "experimenters" (those who have experienced imminent death), do not speak of "rcturn to life", but of "rebirth", they have discovered the "beyond" of life. They have been completely transformed.

The doubt

There are moments in our lives when we feel most vulnerable, it is necessary to take control of ourselves, to overcome difficulties, it requires a strong mind, if it happens to you, to ask yourself why you have taken so much trouble to give up immediately, it is not worth giving up, you have to go ahead with your projects, no matter what the end result, you have to go ahead and start again as many times as necessary, do not let your dreams go by your doubts.

The human being is fascinating and complex , who sometimes has paradoxical thoughts, does not always think in a linear way, is a mind deviated and wandering by nature. In the relationship with those around him, he looks for qualities that others do not have at first, and after a while, they find the defects that others have.

If you took the time to sit down and think about yourself, take a deep breath and look around you right now, you would realize that there is nothing dramatic about it. If you think about life, it just runs its course and there can be good things and bad things, just be careful.

On the cusp of a personal creation, when you are almost there, the seed of doubt is created, it is like declaring your love to someone, when you reach the threshold of your door, you feel that you are deflating, your legs stagger, your thoughts get confused, the walls rise against you and you no longer seem to move forward. The easiest way would be to avoid the problem, wait a little to be in better shape to move forward, but when?

Doubt will remain in this sweet stranger, you will do nothing to know his true face, there is no joy or disappointment, you are enclosed in your little consolation of ignorance, because deep down, if you do not take the step, you will never know. The obstacles are in your head, sometimes you just have to lower your head, even if that means getting slapped, but that's life. And the further we go, the more blows we receive, and the stronger we become.

To put into practice what I said, I'm going to launch some mini challenges, starting little by little, from the things that are within your reach, to those that are less, the goal is to go step by step.

The imagination

Depending on how you have lived, you have accumulated a lot of information in your life, both in terms of social environment and learning, the imagination takes shape.

If you have few tools, you improvise with what you have. There are socio-cultural codes of which you have little or no knowledge. Your mind can only give you some answers, but it doesn't know them all, you must have the initiative to give it "matter".

You have to be curious about everything, read books, watch documentaries, go to painting exhibitions, talk to artists, feed your mind, order everything, and while you sleep, rethink your days, everything you have learned and continue to learn is like pieces of a puzzle that come together to shape a project. Be eager for curiosity, even if you don't like going to certain places, go there anyway, you will probably lack elements for the realization of your projects.

Impressions of "Déjà vu"

We've often thought of places we don't know exist, or described where they are, or moved to places that activate a click, feeling like we've been there before.

Scientifically, these impressions of "déjà vu" are triggered by electrical stimuli in our brain, the human body has a low energy charge to make it work, but what causes these stimuli?

Everyone can move from their beliefs, some of which seem eccentric, to the belief supporters of parallel worlds, it would seem that we move to the same place as our "other us", either in the moment or in the past. For others, it is a point of confluence of our destiny, it is precisely here where we should be, although I do not subscribe so much to these theories, it continues to provoke reflection.

The destiny

No one is really doomed to fate. Nobody stands in the way, destiny is never written in stone, except in their imagination, we can control it, their only way to survive is in our state of mind, it is our thoughts that make us take one path instead of another, with the complicity of false beliefs rooted in your subconscious, the same that has shaped how you react to situations.

Far from it, I would say that we are responsible for our destiny, but it is the result of an accumulation of erroneous thoughts in our youth, if it is understood correctly, everything is linked to how we were educated and how we live afterwards.

The past has shaped our present, which makes us make decisions that may or may not be catastrophic, so doing nothing is also a choice, think about it!

We are all identical in one aspect, having received an education, parental, academic, relational or professional.

What have certain situations brought us, to meet people or situations that guide our choices according to our acquired convictions and our emotions of the moment, going from the stage of anger to enthusiasm, we can believe in happy accidents, in the providence that we must take advantage of, as well as in the tiles and the bad omen that we must avoid, but how can we differentiate the two if our interpretation of these concepts is false?

Everything is a matter of choice according to our mood of the moment, those we were doing determine our present, then one thing leads to the other, draws or caricatures our future.

They have never really been masters of their destiny because of what they have learned since the beginning of their existence.

The end of life

For you, there is still time to act, or to remain fearful of the future that will come if you do nothing about it, when we approach retirement and turn around on the road we have traveled, we feel that we have had a good life for the most part, but for others, they spend the end of their lives groaning with mental feedback, they live in immense sadness, in three quarters of the cases alone in an apartment or retreat house where there is not a living soul. Your last vision is not that of your successful child(ren), but that of the nurse or doctor who came to accompany you, shaking the hand of an illustrious stranger.

If you haven't planned anything for that, do it! There are death insurance policies that I took out very early, it's not a question of age, we can die very young (incurable illness or accident). The most difficult part when we come to the end of our existence, a question remains open, what will we leave behind? Any problem? Any debt? Who will remember us?

We must act here and now, not tomorrow, or within a month, the action of your existence is happening now! Over the years, death will not wait for you to make up your mind. If you don't want to repent anymore, do it! Succeed or fail, but move!

Self-acceptance

Whether your past, your social environment, your education or your environment, is your life, learn to love yourself as you are without creating another character. They are your foundation and it is from there that they have to build themselves, and without a foundation, nothing makes sense. Reconsider your life in a better light, find strengths in weaknesses, and later you will have the pleasure of contemplating your past by being proud of the progress you have made. Love one another and appreciate what you have.

Passivity of emotions

Passivity refers to a person in the absence of all emotions, and without them, there is no passion, and without passion, there is no inspiration.

Perhaps you have resigned yourself to living your daily life without taste, sitting on your couch and watching TV shows that confuse your brain. It all comes down to the subway, work, sleep and nothing else. The cause is resignation, you're so depressed you seem to be having trouble getting up.

Go out for a while, see the outside world, see how beautiful it is, breathe and feel everything around you! Don't get caught up in your vicious circle, do something new! Describe to me how you feel using your five senses.

Right now, I'm on my terrace writing these lines, there's a beautiful blue sky, it's May 2018, there's little noise outside, cars are rolling, there's a cup of coffee on the table, I'm quite relaxed, serene, for the moment, I'm just writing my writings, I find ideas recalling moments I've lived recently, a dispute, a moment of reconciliation, words spoken, even negatives events inspire me, make me strong, and with a slight smile, even my cat inspires me. When we search hard, inspiration is everywhere in everyday life, in good times and bad.

Speaking of "cat", it inspires me more, in my youth, I read a book by Ernest Hemingway, you would say to me "*what is the connection?*"

Ernest Hemingway was what we might call an "ailurophile" (those who love cats) like many authors, including Colette. He had over a hundred in his home in Key West, Florida, today it's a museum where live permanently many cats of the lineage of the author, also liked to go fishing, was another of his passions.

From his passions came inspiration, he moved, he traveled, he met people, if he was stayed at home, his inspiration would still be there, but it would be boring.

When I was a teenager, I was in fifth grade, the other students and me have studied a book by this author called "The Old Man and the Sea", when we are young, generally think of something more than reading, quite entertaining and less in line with the environment of the book, very uninspired, I must say.

Who would have thought that one day, and now, I would read about fifty pages a day, or one book a week? Do the math in a year!

What I lacked was "the fiber", the desire to read, I saw it as something boring, but in the end, I appreciate each story, I spend one or two hours a day in it, it's nothing for 24 hours.

Reading, beyond teaching me things, has also allowed me to escape from my daily life. It made me feel emotions from which passion was born, and passion is inspiration.

What gave you the biggest emotions in your life? Fall in love? Go to an amusement park and ride a roller coaster? Or anything else?

I have already experienced great emotions of love, fear and strength, we find emotions everywhere, and one of the ones that gives me the most is the ocean, the storm and the rough sea,

I remember the feeling when I went to Lake Geneva, near Thononon, in Haute-Savoie, in October 2003, although I went there several times, it was at that very moment when I felt many emotions.

There weren't many people that day, only a few spectators, it contrasted well with the lively city I met in summer with its coffee terraces full of people, foreign tourists from all over the world, Germany, Italy or England, sometimes I had fun guessing the nationalities of tourists listening to them speak, if they didn't speak, they were upper class (I joked, of course). At the docks, there were sellers of costume jewellery, ice cream and summer pastries, and even toys for children, such as water pistols.

But the life inspired by Thonon in summer becomes a feeling of death, an emptiness that settles in me. Returning to the period I was talking about, October 2003, I cannot explain why I felt a strong emotion when I saw the agitation of the water and the strong wind blowing towards me, which made me breathe an air that left me breathless. Looking far away, on the horizon, I felt an emptiness, my thoughts were lost in the distance, I felt small in front of the elements, in front of the immensity of the lake, inspired fear and something insurmountable, and I wanted to defy the storm. On the docks, there were sailboats, the beating of the wind on the trembling masts, and the snapping of the carabiners colliding with each other.

The place where I live is a great source of inspiration, there are some for all kinds of people, for those who like paragliding, hang-gliding, ballooning, swimming, or just walking through the forest.

The Anger Trap

It is one of the seven deadly sins, it is easy to succumb to it when someone really irritates us, because of our ego and pride.

When an individual comes to you angry, let him do it and control your emotions, of course, you will be tempted to "calm him down", to show your muscles feeling offended, you want him to respect you, but what would it be like to be considered impulsive or violent? It would only make the situation worse, two conflicting negative forces, create sparks and risk absorbing some of their negative energy.

The solution? Remain calm and maintain your positive energy, speak calmly to reduce tensions, do not run away, face him and show that you are not afraid of him, speak calmly, the object of discord will find a favorable result. If you listen to him, get away from his point of view. Of course, nothing prevents you from defending yourself if necessary, but if you don't need to fight, don't!

Habits and whims

Since we were very young, we've maintained certain habits, good or bad, that's not the point, they've led you to where you are now.

From my point of view, it is difficult, if not impossible, to embark on a project with a large pinion containing anger, doubt, bitterness and fear, and a small pinion containing wisdom, patience, faith and enthusiasm. Your positivity will soon be clear, unless you change your lifestyle.

What we call Lubies are deliberate repetitions, that is, starting projects on impulse and then giving up after a while. Getting rid of it must go through a form of self-discipline, if we spend our lives always changing our opinion, we have nothing in the end, we must meet clear objectives. If you find it too complicated, ask yourself why it is so difficult and how I can achieve this goal, the answer is simple, changing yourself, both in your habits and in your ways of thinking.

If you start a project knowing that there are limitations, it is as if you want to accelerate by applying the brake.

The famous "yes, but" and "if".

If my project doesn't succeed?
What if they don't take me seriously?
Yes, but I need money.

Yes, but what if clients are not interested in my project?
Yes, but how can we do this in an existing market?

Then, with this kind of thinking, you will not get anywhere, because it is full of discouragement, you make a very bad estimation of yourself and your real abilities. Remember that if people have been successful, you can do it, you have to chase away the "demon of dis-motivation" within you!

You are trapped in your own thoughts, consciously or unconsciously, you make an endless loop, no matter what the circumstances. Look where you are now, have your decisions led you to success? If you read me, I doubt it (unless it's just a reader's curiosity and you've found my book by pure chance).

You make the same pattern all the time, conditions and environment are different, but the rest is the same. When you make a decision about a problem, you put it into action, which causes a reaction, if it is positive at first, it becomes negative later, bringing you back to the same point, and with another problem. Your daily life is about that, you start cycles again, even correcting the situation, nothing will work, because you have your thought system, your golden idol, your false beliefs.

How to force the psychological mechanisms? Changing our habits.

One of the reasons the power of attraction doesn't affect you is that you probably expect it to work, there is a certain amount of excess insurance on it.

It's like being an electrician when we're plumbers. If our knowledge allows us to replace a simple light bulb ore an electrical outlet, you can do it too, there are only two wires, but few people know how to name them, some say "it's easy, there's a + and a -", but what's the + and what's the -? What's the red color for? What's its function?

In 1993, I joined CECAM at Saint Jeoire in Haute-Savoie, where I was able to learn four trades, including electricity, and I learned to name electrical cables, the red that designates "phase" (the +) and the blue that designates "neutral" (the -), and that depending on the type of alternating or direct current, in a house, for example, we could alternate, but not in a car battery.

There are categories of people who say "I know! I've seen it! "but they are incapable of reproducing what they have seen with precision.

To build an engine, you have to know how to name the pieces, know their functions and not build it in "I've seen it done" mode, but it is the resonance of most individuals who launch projects, but who "make a lot of mistakes" from the beginning.

Too much insurance in everyday life is a trap we can all fall into, being too sure of something doesn't necessarily mean it works.

Study your life plan carefully, act in the present moment without worrying about the future, because it is built into every act we do.

Golden Rules

- Prepare the ground in your subconscious, do not compromise without changing your mood. And let it go when you feel ready.

- Do not change your behavior abruptly, do it little by little to give time to those around you to assimilate it, otherwise it would be a shock or a surprise.

- Don't project yourself too much on your goal to reach with a sense of victory, that's the trap, you'd risk spending too much energy to be disappointed in the end.

- Just do it!, take notes, make diagrams and a life plan , create algorithms (logical sequences of things to do daily).

- Act in your thoughts as if the object of your desires were already acquired.

CHAPTER 3: THE INTERNAL AND EXTERNAL ENVIRONMENT

There are two types of environment, the first is within you, it is your essence, your thoughts, your perception of the world, and the second is around you, what others think or say, your family, your friends, acquaintances, the social environment, whether you are in the city or in the countryside.

Your vibratory field

It brings together two forms of energy, one positive and one negative, both enclosed in a bubble, and vibrates in harmony with the outside world, we can also attribute it to a certain expression, "to be in its bubble" which means to be in its world, it contains your dreams, your imagination, your fears, your doubts and all other feelings. When you keep everything to yourself, within this vibratory field, nothing happens outside to those you may encounter.

Living in osmosis with your dreams bringing you inner well-being is not enough and will not change anything in your condition if there is no interaction with the world outside your bubble, no one will know what is happening inside you if you don't let nobody to enter into your secret garden.

You have built a fortress of fears and doubts around this vibratory field, all positive feelings are enclosed in it, so we must say that you are a closed person, unfortunately this is felt by others.

Also be very careful with what you take out of your vibratory field, the two positive and negative energies can intertwine.

We must be interested in others, not because I tell you in this book, but because you are part of a "whole," that is, the intercommunication of energies flowing through others and yourself. You have to be interested in others in a disinterested way, forget your personal expectations, get this out of your mind, send waves of impatience to your interlocutor.

"It's better to live your dreams than to dream your life."
(François Garagnon)

You have to externalize your dreams, even if it means ruining them, but let them express themselves, don't keep everything to yourself in the shadows of regrets.

A famous Belgian singer named Jacques Brel spoke in one of his video interviews about "postponement", it was in the mid-1970s, in this interview he told the story of an individual who wanted to write a book, but before that, he should to sell pickles, and then, after that, he will start writing. Two years later, he met this same person, who said: "I finished selling my pickles, now I sell suspenders, but after that, I write a book. Jacques Brel had a laught about this situation in this video, because we're all a bit like that, always postponing until the next day, and then until the next day. His conclusion is as follows: "suspenders or pickles, beyond of that, if we have dreams, we must realize them, and take the risk of crashing! »

If the path to success were summarized in several steps, they would be as follows:

To try, no matter the result, the important thing is not to succeed the first time, otherwise, the disappointment is great, there is no projection into the future, only the present moment, what you do now will determine your future, the essential is "to do", "Just do it!".

(as a famous brand of shoes would say), as well that you don't try to succeed at all costs the first time, do it! It's very simple!

To fail,learn from your mistakes and do not live them as a fatality, when you believe in your dreams, everything is possible. If you are the only ones who believe in it, make lie the statistics that called you losers.

To get up, even though you seem trapped in quicksand, keep on advancing, the promised land is not far away, perhaps a few meters away. Fall and start again, take advantage of your mistakes in the process.

To keep an eye on the horizon, has a goal to achieve and will achieve it if you does not stop on the way. It is your goal and not the goal of others, do not let anyone divert you from your path.

To understand yourself

Who are you really? I speak to you in terms of behavior in relation to life, are you of the critical, respectful, economic, spending type, you complain all the time, you take life with philosophy, in every little moment of the day, you tell yourself that everything is going to be better after the storm.

Analyze yourself first, you'll find some answers to your problems.

Why you can't make ends meet, is it because you don't earn enough or are spending money without realizing it?

If you feel uncomfortable at work, is it your colleagues' fault, or are you the one who makes you be judged? You could also break down open doors.

In all this, I come to a central point, what if the real problem was you?

If you want to understand your illness, you have to find its symptoms!

In the other sense, of course there are people who will judge you, but you shouldn't give so much importance to what they say, you just value who you are!

For my part, trye to say it in yourself, you have courage, imagine that I am in front of you saying this and encouraging you, YOU ARE A ABLE OF MANY THINGS AND VALES

MUCH MORE THAN YOU BELIEVE VALES. and you can become a better version of yourself. Learn to accept yourself as you are, Love yourself first!

If you do the work on yourself, you will be amazed at all the changes that can occur in your life.

TRUST YOURSELF!

In the previous chapter, I discussed with you the issue of cyclicals, which is not insignificant, it is about making you aware of what inexorably pushes you towards failure.

Whether you like it or not, you are drawn into an infernal spiral, whatever your actions, the consequences will be the same, the time of the revolution of the little whirlwind that represents the positive energies will remain minimal, establishing good relations with people, having an easy dialogue, talking about things and others with strangers is a good training base. Without dialogue, it is difficult to make oneself known, especially in the business world, where big bosses have to pick up the phone every day. So practice that.

First of all, you have to be good to others and vice versa.

If you do not resolve point by point what happens to you and your habits, it is to replace a bad habit by a good one, thus reducing the volume of the vicious circle, save time, there will be a clear improvement in your behavior and that of others towards you, situations will always find a favorable result.

Ask yourself these questions! What do you do every day? What are your priorities for life and the environment? Is it your past that bothers you?

There is a certain perception of the world around us, of how we feel it, a psychological interpretation of this or that individual(s). You have probably experienced a form of parental authority, a particular education, quotes that have had an influence on your mind.

Are you one of those who will be recognized in this description?

In the evening, our character returned to his low-rent housing neighborhood, where there were visible towers on the other side of the city and whose antennas seem to touch the sky.

He drove in his old car whose mileage was being felt, fatigue on the one hand when he got home from work, and fear on the other when he returned home wondering what people he would meet. He parked his car, checked that his vehicle was locked, avoided glances, and entered his building.

He closed the door with two turns and turned on the television while sitting on his sofa, with a cup of coffee in his hand to "release his tensions" (supposedly). He watched the news announcing that the unemployment rate had risen again, then immersed himself in the evening film showing the violence, our character was absorbed, concentrated, while ignoring that what he saw was playing with his psychic, because the violence he saw on television was actually found on the outside.

Your brain is a database accumulated throughout our lives, followed by your emotional states at this very specific time.

What I mean by that, given what you've been through, is that you need a reprogramming of your brain to move from a dominated position to a dominant one.

In this chapter we will study the strengths and weaknesses (that can become strengths), in order to determine the origin of the blockages, it can be less exciting to talk about the past, but it is necessary to do a background treatment.

To do this, we will look back, because it is about YOU. I will teach you to straighten out and gain confidence, and without going through this step, it wouldn't all make sense. In your life, everything has been mended like a vase in which we put glue stitches, its beauty has been altered.

To understanding others and what surrounds us

The first thing to do is to be interested in others and their vibratory field, to break their shells and send positive waves, to be careful, without the need to force, would risk that their interlocutor appears and becomes impermeable to their words.

Once their shells are broken, this person will trust you and listen to you, otherwise you will have to win it first.

Do not present yourself too much, let your interlocutor ask you questions, answer them with the greatest sincerity, open your heart.

We all need a full understanding of the world around us, to see people living and have their happiness that seems inaccessible to you, but are you sure these people are happy at home?

They can hide their sadness when they leave their homes to change their mind, one of the lessons to be learned is that you cannot trust appearances, you also see it in people who seem poorer than you. In your opinion, can they be happy? If they are satisfied only with the rags they use, without worrying about success, at least they have a different perception of success.

I say this because in most countries of aboriginal culture, which have developed without knowing our civilization, they are told about computers or other technologies, it is foreign to their culture. What they have makes them rich, which means that we all have a different perception of wealth. This is explained by a phenomenon of "cultural sufficiency", they don't need more, because they don't know they can have more.

When I was still in high school, I studied Maslow's pyramid, which meets all the needs that have to be satisfied to achieve their full personal development.

This pyramid is built in stages, with the so-called "physiognomic" needs at its base, man needs to drink, eat and dress to live. On the second level, we have security needs. The marginalized are at this level and cannot access the floor above which the needs of belonging to a community are grouped.

Ignorance of the possibility of obtaining beyond this level means that some cultures are satisfied with this third level and already imagine themselves to be at the top.

Then comes the need for self-esteem, to know how we perceive ourselves and in relation to others, are we appreciated or not? It is largely our behavior toward others that determines who we are, because those we encounter reflect what we show them.

When we reach the top of this pyramid, we have achieved (or almost) all our goals, we are in full self-realization, we have achieved a prosperous life and a very good comfort of life. The "or almost" means that you should not rest on your laurels and keep up, otherwise you will fall apart.

At what level are you?

In fact, you are in the third level for the vast majority, and in the fourth level for others.

This is explained by our subconscious security mechanism, a way of saying that you are very well where you are, so why do you want more? I will answer you, because all of you can do it. But you haven't taken enough out of yourself.

Put aside all your past beliefs, don't let yourself be absorbed by "that's what they say", don't compare yourself with others, because you are all unique.

I understand the difficulties you have had in getting to where you are, but deep down, is that what you really want?

You are paralyzed by the fear of losing everything by throwing the dice, stopping working to establish your own business seems to be a risky business. All this because they have taught you to give up, they have flooded you with everything you can see or hear on

114

television, on the radio, in the newspapers that talk about wars and poverty.

The first and most important thing is to learn to have confidence in oneself.

The hierarchy

One of the reasons would also come from the importance you give to others. The origin of these thoughts would come from your childhood when you saw that adults were "naturally" tall in front of you, when you saw them as authority figures, you felt diminished.

When adults didn't take you seriously in your projects, even in your teens, teachers, school principals always kept this authority and superiority in you. Over the years, this superiority that inspired you was rooted in you.

During your internship, if you have ever done one, these authoritative figures gave you a sense of fear. But tell yourself that this feeling of fear, they also had it when they were younger, and almost nothing differentiates you from them except their studies and their ability to free themselves. They had the opportunity to have role models and a conscious mind, open to the world.

What may impress you is the age, the bank account, the diplomas and the wardrobe, on the other hand it is possible to dismantle all these limiting beliefs by telling you that you will arrive one day as old as they (almost certainly, but I put a reservation on it because we can die young unfortunately), then, you can save according to your possibilities, then, the diplomas help, but some people do it without (self-taught), and finally, the suit is not necessarily synonymous with success, I wear it on all occasions and the prices have become very affordable.

What brings you closer to the hierarchy is that we all die, rich or poor, what can make us different are the circumstances of our burial, ending up in a mass grave or in a fir box with gold handles.

Qualities and defects

When I was in the formation of NLP in 2004 at the Chamber of Commerce and Industry, I remember that the speaker mentioned in his course that "defects can be qualities, and qualities can be defects".

Don't you believe it?

When you feel the best, the strongest, the most intelligent, etc., you create a vibratory field around you so that you can see others inferior to you and not like your peers, never forget that each individual you know is a reflection of yourself.

Put yourself in your place, have the ability to put yourself in the place and feelings of your interlocutor, what we can also call "having the external eye".

How do you think they perceive you? As arrogant, pretentious and proud beings, you make them feel these feelings.

When you are in a state where what you feel is a misjudgment of their qualities, whether you feel inferior or null, you make them feel just by seeing yourself.

Some will try to help you, accept their help, we still need others, there is nothing dishonorable about it, and stop thinking you are incapable, it's the poison of your existence.

You're normal and you're fine with your slippers despite the circumstances. Learn to be impassive to your weaknesses, don't show them, and be strong in your convictions, always smile and be happy.

I have been working with a smile on my face that surprised many people, because circumstances did not lend themselves to it! A ton of work was extending my arms. So what? Nobody is superhuman, despite the pressure of my employer, I did my work silently, and the ease with which I applied it made me finish what I had to do the same as if I was stressed, the difference is that I was less tired.

Passivity in my case has been a quality, not being overwhelmed by events, is completely useless and can interrupt your work.

the magnetism of a person

We often talk about someone's attractiveness, but what about him?

We all have an energy capital from birth and a toolbox in our mind, every time we go through a situation, we always have a choice, which is human nature, when someone irritates us, for example.

We have the opportunity to listen to it or ignore it, to tell ourselves that this individual is unhappy.

What if we tried to give this person some of our energy? Would it be less unhappy or harmful?

Offer a rose to a woman and she will thank you, on the contrary, if she is too bitter, she will say "I don't want your flower".

Therefore, there are two possibilities for you, either to reason in such a way that you say "too bad for you", or to understand why she don't want it, to let it express itself without interpreting, she must feel that you capture its attention, that person will perceive you as someone who listens, who is altruistic, who doesn't try to justify himself, nor to present himself. Capture this energy with kindness, it will grow in you, the more you do good around you, and the more you will be appreciated.

The energy is in you and in everyone you meet

Have you ever noticed when you feel uncomfortable or in the presence of someone? This individual shows his magnetism, without you having to know him, despite what he does or is.

The environment in which we live is part of a whole, of each being, of each plant, of each animal, unconsciously, we communicate with each other, to give you some examples, when you have a song in mind, have you ever noticed that a person next to you hums it? Or when you look at a person behind you, you see them turn and look at you? It's the same when you feel observed, turn your head and, in fact, someone is looking at you.

I have thought of one person in particular, I met her recently, and yet I had a very clear vision in my dreams, carrying her in my arms and in a wedding dress, now she lives with me. Some will say that it is a premonition, but the intentions were shared, she told me that she saw me in her dreams.

Your environment reflects in you what you send them, ie the bad waves, accumulate within you, the more charged the polarity and stronger is the attraction, both positive and negative. The secret is there, do good around you! Do not give a disastrous image by constantly criticizing, insulting or complaining.

That's why it's important to keep your thoughts healthy, to do little things to make someone smile, to say "hello", "thank you", "how are you? "show your interest in others and they will give it back to you.

Here you will find one of the doors to the attraction of your emotional and material desires.

Encourage young people to pass their exams, wish them happiness or health, make sure they smile and are widely appreciated.

The waves that people will send you will accumulate in you (many will say "yes, but it doesn't work"), something very important, let things come naturally, without waiting for them to come, go to your business, make gestures or words of kindness or attention, and then forget your expectations of a return. This will be done gradually without forcing.

The Domino Theory

Each action leads to another, what is also called a chain reaction and also depends on the decisions we make in life, not everything is doomed to failure, only if we give up, and we are where we are, either we take the risk of tearing down the following dominoes, or we remain in uncertainty, it is also to become aware and accept that we can fail, what will give us the path to follow, perhaps another failure, may last five times, a hundred times, even beyond.

When you give up, you don't know what's behind the domino.

The decisions you make for your future are as uncertain as Schrödinger's cat.
Locked in a box, you don't know the result, and you don't risk going any further upstream.

Learn to take risks, don't limit yourself to your fears, cross that line, have confidence, what will happen, but don't be discouraged.

As I said, your actions have taken you to where you are now, there is nothing negative to conclude, life always gives you the opportunity to bounce, what blocks you is that you have learned to abandon, your existence has been an accumulation of hard blows, so what? Accept what you have become and push the next domino.

Each action has a consequence, what you do today determines what you will be tomorrow, the world is always in motion, whether you do something or not, in your stagnation or in your initiative.

Wealth or poverty are not synonymous with success or failure

The environment has no social status, whether we are rich or poor, it depends on how our beliefs are from birth, and how we are educated.

In the case of a child born into a rich family, his father is a businessman and earns a living, prospers, enough to protect him and his whole family from need, while the child teaches him not to be afraid of the future because he has everything he wants from life, lives in a cocoon. His father is often absent on business trips and does not have time to devote to the education of his son, to the transmission of his knowledge, his mother is too protective with him and watches over his schooling. This child has the social rank that favours him, without worrying at all about education, he is a rebellious young man. A few years later, he will not be able to take over his father's business and will benefit from a very beautiful inheritance without knowing what to do with it, because he did not have the transmission of knowledge.

In the case of a child born into a poor family, if in adulthood he has a reason to accept his condition, when he decides to fight his way out of it (if he has one), he will create a new culture of life that should have been forged since childhood, he will have accumulated so much suffering, so much fear, so much doubt that it will be difficult for him to take the right path, but that does not mean impossible.

Ego and bad faith

We all have an ego, excessive or not, consciously or unconsciously, but we act mainly for ourselves, looking closer, what exactly do you expect from the people around you? Satisfaction? Recognition? Love?

Analyze your own behavior with others, surrender unconditionally or wait to receive you too? When you offer something, do it with your heart, don't expect any merit, let go of your expectations of receiving in return.

124

Live in the rhythm of the world around you without blaming anyone, accept that someone is more educated than you and others less, that some go faster than you, and others slower. Recognize that you do not have infuse science, you simply live in harmony with the world around you.

In other words, if you want to get close to the person you want, you need to get close to the conditions required for it.

The only way to have blindness is in your objectives, and no one has the absolute truth, not you, not me, not your relatives, not even the corrector who breaks his head with my current text. Only God has this power.

This was the case of the directors of a company whose name, place and date I would not mention, for the simple reason that I worked for them, and that I do not want to be on the side of the equivalent of Mr. Dupont-Moretti to defend myself (a famouse french lawyer) .

This structure called *** did not have any benefit, it was rather on the descending slope, however, the leaders did everything possible to improve working conditions, put paint on the right and left, filled holes in the ground, even rebuilt the toilets and invested a lot in machines and other technical means.

However, the company found it difficult to take off, customers got tired and went to see if the grass was greener elsewhere. There were criticisms, many team meetings, that we had to produce more, that we had to pay attention to the quality of our work, that we had to be accused of all evils, that we had to be threatened with dismissal, etc.......

Despite all this, nothing came, and the managers wondered why the employees were not involved in the company.

The reason is very simple, they only saw their personal interests and perceived the employees as interchangeable objects, putting a sword of Damocles in their head, they only spoke of the difficulties of the company, of why they were not making profits, because the essential "human relations" were missing.

The leaders sent negative waves, did not listen to the problems of their employees, a generator of stress and anxiety creating depression, if the man is a mirror for the man, they were not listened to.

Too much to think about their sales, profits, customers, have forgotten that for a company to work, everyone must work as a team, employees must be recognized and valued, otherwise the "I don't care" and bitterness is opposed to that of their superiors.

And when I talk about recognition, it's not just about shaking hands when taking office, or organizing outings or Christmas celebrations, nothing to do, really, is to be recognized as human, encourage, say you're doing a good job, everyone has to belong to a group and be valued.

While superiors only saw employees as inferior beings to those who preached, they created a bad environmental climate, a "stinking" atmosphere of negativity that had a direct impact on the quality of work, on production and, later, on customers. All they lacked was coaching (I'll come back to that later), the power to push employees towards positivity, and that must continue to make staff happy to come to work and be proud of their company.

Convincing others

One observation that has been made many times over the years is that some individuals are closed-minded. Despite their knowledge and studies, some people find an unfounded truth in their subconscious.

Even for us, we sometimes persevere in error, compartmentalized into an unconscious system of thoughts, refusing to acknowledge our deficiencies and ignorance about certain subjects.

The most skillful would even be able to make us swallow snakes, to convince you that something is true when it is not. It also depends on how you are perceived and that, according to them, you are constantly in error, it is not your knowledge that they attack, but your person, and ideally, it would be better to escape from these toxic and narcissistic individuals.

When you say that the color is green, your interlocutor will reply that it is light green or blue, wanting to add a precision to stand out, although the truth is absolute, you will want to keep "reason" and control placed over you.

Or that we are, in the field of everyday life, political or professional, as you say, the answers are of the type "But no, you won't! "or "the meeting was well organised, but it could have been better".

It is difficult to get someone to accept your ideas depending on how you are perceived. Appearance and speech play an important role. One remedy to overcome this phenomenon is to accept what others say, even if the other person is still wrong. Because his mind, like all others, is in selfishness, we all want to be right in what we do and say, whatever the individual.

Helping others

Assistance exists in two forms, "help" in a selfless way, and in another slightly more selfish aspect, personal, either consciously or unconsciously.

Unconsciously, we do it in everyday life, when you shop, when you go to work, you contribute with someone else, always. If you wonder where your salary comes from, it's clear it comes from the boss, but who pays the boss? It is through the sale of your company's products that you are paid, and who is the buyer? It can be you or someone else, if I take the example of a brand of peas (an example that often appears in the economy, who knows why!), if you work in the factory that makes them, nothing prevents you from buying one of the boxes in the supermarket. Then, when you take another brand, you contribute to the remuneration of another person like you. When you buy the latest Iphone or an HDTV to please yourself, you please someone else. That's what I would call unconscious assistance.

We can be altruistic without believing that we are altruistic, so we must study deeply within ourselves and ask ourselves the question, if we help you, who are we really doing it for? To be glorified or noticed, or for a selfless and free purpose?

When we meet a person in difficulty, of course we can help him, but when he doesn't understand why he is in difficulty, in spite of our advice and support, he continues on his way, at first he says he has learned the lesson, but in the end, some time later, we find this same individual in the same situation as before, it's almost sad.

There are beings on this earth who can drown in difficulties, without taking any teaching of what has happened in their lives. I wonder if this is not part of their culture of life.

The lesson to be learned is that you too are responsible for their conditioning, simply because for this person, you become like a horn of abundance from which he can draw, the problem is that "you are there! "and live in the present moment of your presence.

No matter what the difficulties, your good heart will lose you, but there is a way to help these people, and that is to give no help, no, no help. You have to put them against the wall, you have to shake them in the mind, you have to feel alone in this situation and you have to be aware of it.

When for her, all this seems to be assimilated (at least, hopefully), you can come back and help them "partially" to get back on track.

This applies to everyone, understanding the difficult times of life and taking responsibility for their consequences.

Learn to step aside from time to time to think about yourself, sacrifice your life for others, focus on your future and your plans, and step away from these "toxic" individuals, whether family or friends, which does not excuse their abandonment of themselves and how they make you feel guilty when you're not there for them.

To serve with a good heart, who knows what that really means? Remember! the man is a mirror for the man (or for the woman, let's not be chauvinists!), and the gift of self must be a totally gratuitous act, that is, once the action of rendering the service has been carried out, it must be immediately forgotten, never think about it again.

I met a person at my job who came to do me a favor without me asking him, I let him do it, but there was no real reason to come and help me.

One day he came to see me to tell him a crazy story and said, "Remember! I did you a favor with all my heart! "I was a little surprised by his words and I simply answered, "So why do you come to complain about it? "It's because he wanted it and not because I asked for it, there are nuances.

In other words, to do an action with a good heart, either you do it without reproaching it afterwards, or you don't do it. No one is obliged to us in this particular case.

It is also what also gets stuck, not doing anything to satisfy yourself, but to please others, the laws of attractiveness are precise, if you don't want to do something for free, then don't do it.

You have understood, the laws of attraction do not work when we are too individualistic, act with karma, never forget this principle "to give to others is to give yourself", when you offer a gift, it is as if this gift were for you, you put yourself in its place and feel its happiness. Unlike when you do it in the hope of getting something in return, it is your ego that expresses itself, that alters your karma. If there is a return, it will happen without even thinking about it, it is called the last moment, when things arrive without delay, sometimes at critical moments.

Basically, lending 20 € to someone, for example, is like lending the same amount in exchange, if you claim it, or if you imagine that if you give this amount to make the laws of attractiveness react, it won't work, you have to forget completely! It is when you no longer think about it that everything happens.

If I have anything else to add on the subject, without looking too much at it, when we want to help others, it is whether the help is disinterested, but also, if someone asks us to do it. I said earlier that, in most cases, the best way to help them is precisely not to do so, especially if nothing is asked of them. An apprentice needs to work on his logical mind, if someone is always behind him telling him how to do something, he will do it in a robotic way without knowing why or how. That's how I trained during one of my internships in a company, my internship supervisor let me work on the problem and, with perseverance, did it. My trainer was very tough, but very fair and I would never thank him enough. In practice, that's how you get "experience".

Pascal the big brother

We need to have an external and self-critical eye to understand what is wrong, not everyone has seen this program on television, maybe it no longer exists at the time of reading these lines, however, there are videos on the Internet that you can see if you are interested.

"Pascal the Big Brother" was a television series that told the story of families in distress because of rebellious children or teenagers who made it difficult for their parents or relatives.

Their role was to refocus these troubled young people, having the "king child" syndrome.

Each situation was different, a father absent, children too spoiled, parents too weak morally, etc. What happened in some episodes was that the children were convinced that they were right, that they were in real life and that their parents were to blame.

So, to bring them back to reality, Pascal took these young people and their families to the green, away from everyday life, where he began a "reframing" therapy.

In some episodes of the program, we were able to see Pascal taking these families to a cinema where people from outside their situation, complete strangers trapped in the street, had taken their seats.

The film began, the child or teenager saw the scenes of his violence and rediscovered himself to his surprise before his face broke, has

135

trouble realizing it was him in the film. What he lacked was an external eye. Criticisms from the audience in the room soon followed, causing further electroshock.

Look at yourself and have an external eye imagining how others see you. Take a tape recorder and record yourself, better than that, make a video, observe your attitude, or ask someone close to you to hide a camera in the room without necessarily explaining its purpose, even if asked questions. What others will be to you will depend on what you are to them!

Be responsible

One of the qualities of a good leader is to know how to take everything on himself, to take responsibility for his actions. What most people do has the unfortunate habit of "delegating" their mistakes, which is observed several times in the workplace, makes people smile even if circumstances do not allow it, when a job is done badly, we blame others,

while if it's well done, we commend its merits.

For example, suppose there's a puddle in the lobby of a collective dwelling, there's traffic, neighbors come and go and realize it's still there, and everyone thinks, "Honestly, someone could have cleaned it up. "Without being one of them, and it is enough that one person decides to take the initiative (the next day), not everyone has this capacity because they say to themselves "I didn't put it there" or "she was already there".

They will have to realize that to be successful, as surprising as it may seem, it must be done through initiatives, to set an example. Unless you are one of those people who watch and do nothing else.

Never ask yourself who did what, as in the example of the puddle, you take it in your hands and pick it up, it would only be for yourself and for your esteem. What others do symbolizes those who do not move forward, such as being caricatured by people working in public works, one digging, and then others observing.

At the bottom of your heart, you accumulate pride for doing each act without delegating, you build your own building from the foundations, you learn to build and you will gain confidence by telling yourself that in the end, it was not so difficult, the point is to try.

Also, don't do anything to make people notice you, but for them to notice you, they must be quite natural gestures. Do you like it when a person congratulates you when you do something with your own hands? The idea seduces you that sprouts in your mind, gives you imagination, and why not practice in this field?

Repeat over and over and welcome all comments with kindness, whether positive or negative. If they are bad, that leaves room for improvement.

I have responded to customer satisfaction surveys, although I was very satisfied with the services, I never gave the highest rating so that the company proposing a survey would not tell itself that everything was fine, so there was no need to improve.

So, to recover from what I was saying, take initiatives, whether good or bad, don't always wait for someone to come and tell you, especially if no one comes.

PART II: HOW TO SOLVE PROBLEMS

CHAPTER 4: PRACTICAL EXERCISES

"I never lose! I win or learn."
(Nelson Mandela)

To regain control, several steps are needed, including learning from the past, rewriting another interpretation of one's own life, and acting in the present for a better future. I will teach you to recalibrate your vibratory field, and tune your internal and external environment to resonate at the same frequency.

Now it's your turn to play!

First exercise

Nothing too complicated, the exercise lasts an hour (you will find the time for it), you just have to sit or lie down in bed (the ideal is the second solution), relax - you and no longer think about the purpose of your life, or external discomfort (an interview that went wrong, a dispute with a colleague, fear of a neighbor, a bill to pay or others). Hands above each other at the height of their heart. No one should be able to interrupt you for x or y reasons, the postman, family or friends should not knock on your door, for example.

Breathe gently through your nose, then exhale through your mouth, while you try to relax, recover your calm, it is very important.

Concentrate only on your breathing and ignore everything else, if your thoughts come back, whether positive or negative, empty your mind by looking at an object in a piece of furniture, the angle of a piece of wall, the mind should be and remain neutral.

When you have released your harmful thoughts and you no longer think about your projects, you are what you could call "in phase", you can incorporate new positive elements (apart from what you really want), imagine that everything is going well around you, do not believe that you will not succeed, because that is exactly what will happen, because you are sending harmful energy to yourself.

In the same way, telling yourself that it is absurd, anything, is too difficult, or the famous "yes, but......". (which you're probably thinking about), until you've tried it, it certainly won't work, while if you try it, it will only cost you one hour of your 24-hour days, you still have 23 left to do what you do.

It is a breathing exercise, the objective is to learn to control the breathing and to be "in phase", to trust in the author who writes this book that in its sense has its utility (that does not do it only to write on the paper), it is not complicated at all, do it, you will thank me later.

I also mentioned the incorporation of positive elements in this state of calm and serenity, which comes from the method of Emile Coué, and I invite you to read his work.

Think of these phrases while you are still breathing:

"Trust yourself! "Everything will be fine", "everything will be fine", "everything will be fine! "Everything is going well now!" "

Try to feel every emotion of well-being, you know? You have the ability to manage your feelings, without forcing, ignoring everything else.

To conclude this first exercise, tell yourself that you are stronger and better than an hour ago, long before this exercise, try to feel a sense of inner greatness, think of your leaders, your boss, all those who are normally above you, tell yourself that you are better than them and that you just have to prove it. Everything can be arranged for you, every day, the sun is and will always be there, behind the clouds and that doesn't matter what happens. It is also important, about how you will behave with others, keep it to yourself! don't talk about it, and keep these thoughts in a corner of your mind.

Second exercise

Take a blank sheet of paper and a pen, and draw a large circle underneath a smaller one. You're going to say, "It's a snowman! "but that's not the point.

These two shapes are his two gears, one positive (the upper) and one negative (the lower).

Draw a horizontal line between these two circles. This represents the "dead center," the place where the energy is neither positive nor negative. When your life is in a "dead center," nothing happens, at least according to popular beliefs, because life is constantly evolving on both sides of the line. A thinker once said, "the only thing that never changes is the change itself.

Above this line, and around the circle, you will notice all the significant and exciting events related to your childhood to date.

For example, it could be family vacations, countries visited, if you've had diplomas, if you've had your driver's license, your love affairs or who you've married, if you have children, etc....

Let go of your inspiration of the moment! You can complete this list when a memory comes to mind.

So far, nothing too bad, but it shows you that in your life you have had victories, even in minor things.

You see, whether you admit it or not now, you have been a winner, more or less great steps that have turned you into the person you are today. So, if you've been a winner in the past, how would it be different today?

Under what circumstances did you get these victories? I give you the secret of unconsciousness.

On a personal level, when I passed my bachelor's degree in accounting, I was consciously not convinced of having it, and unconsciously, there was this repressed desire in my conscience, there were thousands of questions in my mind, including one in particular.

"If I am not convinced that I have my degree, what am I doing here and why have I gone to so much trouble?

I thought of all those who believed in me, and I can assure you that there were not many of them.

About you now, why did you do all this and how would it be different now? About your life or your current environment?

I can guarantee you one thing, it is that in your heart, you have remained the same person, the same child with wide open eyes, and wanting to discover the world.

If you take a moment of the day to think about everything I write to you, a moment of calm, you will close your eyes and try to concentrate on your milestones! It's not just about thinking about memories, it's about imbuing yourself with them - you'll imagine every detail, every circumstance, and every emotion you feel!

When you do this, isolated from today's outside world, calmly, you will experience a sense of well-being. You will find inner strength and say to yourself: "I was strong then". »

I would tell you to do it later after reading the following lines, because I am with you to do some background work.

The following approach is necessary to evolve and I cannot ignore the negative aspects that also constitute your life.

The disappointments of life are opportunities to evolve, nobody would ever have said, not even me, that I would be inspired by bad events to take advantage of them, I thank the people who indirectly helped me to become stronger. You will become impassive and you will not show your weaknesses.

It is possible to take advantage of bad memories, the key is here, to straighten up and ride again after the fall.

Remove the sheet on which you have recorded your significant events!

Below the line, will you notice your most painful memories? Think about the things that made you feel uncomfortable, for example, if in your childhood you hurt someone and now you are consumed by remorse, if people made you suffer, when and why you stopped studying, etc.......

My goal is not to hurt you and make you aware of reality, and make you stronger, you will learn to overcome your pain after this passage. Recognize your mistakes will make you a better person, I explain how.

In the union between the two gears, place a large dot to mark the location. It is time "T" or "reference point", if a gear makes a complete turn (or revolution), it returns to its starting point, time at which ends the event or events to start a complete turn again. A new cycle starts for a more or less long time, the small gear, which represents positive energy, has a short cycle for you. Your enthusiasm decreases when the revolution is complete, in terms of duration, can be of the order of a week to a few months, while on the other side of the line, can be very long, several years before you reach the end of the cycle.

We must be aware that everything has a beginning and everything has an end, an alpha and an omega, there are births and deaths, just as the sun follows the moon, and so on, everything in the universe follows cycles. Yours is on the way, but time is limited, try to use it instead of waiting, because depending on the size of your gears, the transition from one energy to another will take a little time if you have accumulated too much negativity in the past.

Take another sheet of paper, draw a horizontal line like the first one (without the gears, we don't need them right now) and rewrite your answers about the most outstanding and exciting events.

On the first page, you will look for a positive substitute for each painful event, for example, if someone made you suffer, say that this person made you morally stronger, because you survived this bad passage, and for those you abused in your childhood, expect the best for them with all your heart, try to alleviate your conscience. Find a way to put it into perspective, even if it's painful.

Write your positive substitutes on the second sheet and say, "This is the person I want to be, this is the new me, and I have become stronger.

Tear the first sheet into a thousand pieces and throw it away saying, "I'm better than that".

From now on, you will reason this way, you will be able to understand others, swear in your subconscious that you will not become the person you have been and you will start again, to get the best out of what life has to offer you.

For the circle of positive energies to grow and the other to shrink, keep in mind that "you are better than you think", go in this direction, take all events as opportunities to move forward overcoming challenges and notice how often you have felt strong in a notebook.

When in doubt, think in terms of "solutions" rather than "problems.
Never forget that behind the clouds, the sun will always be there, believe in this star and its light.

Third exercise

To see the object of our desires materialize, we must have the ability to harmonize our imagination with the outside world to resonate with the same sound. Your mind must be in tune with what exists, otherwise it would be a lost cause.

Withdraw to the countryside, to the mountain or to the forest, in short, be green, harmonization begins with communion with nature, it is a regenerative source. It is the origin of all that you are.

Sit in a quiet place, away from all external disturbances, sit down and contemplate what surrounds you, listen to the sound of birds, the sound of the forest, feel the cold or heat over you soak up all the elements, the grass, the flowers, the trees, the wind.

Then, once you have engraved all these elements in you, close your eyes and think only of that moment.

Let yourself be overwhelmed by everything around you, inhale and exhale slowly, you are one with your environment. Feel the vibration in you, it is a pure energy.

Love nature, feel this from the bottom of your heart and let this feeling invade your body.

Time no longer exists, your problems are forgotten, there is only you and your environment, you are relaxed.

Open your eyes and contemplate again, look at the horizon and tell yourself that the universe is infinite.

Fourth exercise

There is a way to put your mind in harmony with abundance, so that you can feel it, imagination plays a very important role.

Create your own universe, as if you had a parallel life, two worlds separated by a door.

Allow yourself at least one hour a day, it's not huge, but enough to help you change your mind. Be diligent and disciplined. Maintain a regularity in this exercise that attracts positive energies to you. I can guarantee it works (Guaranteed Success).

In your mind, you will create your own (positive) story, and insert all the elements necessary for your personal development. Not

152

in vain did I ask them to make lists of significant and painful events, and then to replace these events with something positive.

You are currently at home, in your environment not conducive to happiness, find a moment of the day when you will not be disturbed, place yourself in a place isolated from all external disturbances (You can also do it while you sleep).

Try to relax! Close your eyes, clear your mind and set your problems aside for a while (too much thinking will not solve them).

You will enter a state of dreams, you will build the life you wanted, you will make a world where everything you want, you already had it, do not omit any detail, your dreams must be precise, with training, you will be successful, as long as you are disciplined. Feel every emotion of calm and comfort, be enthusiastic as if everything was taken for granted. Breathe slowly, enjoy every moment and let your heart beat at its own pace in your universe.

In this other world, behind the door of your mind, you have everything you've always wanted, a luxury car, a big house, a good job, and you no longer have any worries about the future.

I studied this principle thanks to one of the books I read, called the "switch".

It is a phenomenon of replacement, substituting one thought for another, for example, you have a boss who is always on his back and yells at you (this is an extreme case), try to have another opinion of him in your mind, imagine that he is kind and understanding, gives you less work, explains that at the moment his business is not going well and asks for your support, rewards you and gives you a promotion. Unlikely to happen, you would say to me, the principle is not that his boss becomes nicer in the real world, but that he becomes nicer in yours, in the conception you have made of him, so that you deal with all the positive energy he gives you in your imagination.

The ideal, for a background treatment is to replace in his mind all his past life, to see you as a strong and appreciated person.

This "switch" is your own world, your parallel universe from which you will draw your positivity. It is your "other you", an inexhaustible source of positive energy where you can recharge your batteries, feel every emotion of the moment you are in this universe created in your mind, recharge yourself every day, interact with the people of this world, and your life will be interrupted, you will notice changes around you, in reality, your unconscious will have changed, your behavior will also be noticed on your face, you will be more enthusiastic than before, you will have a smile, and others will see it.

For realism to be optimal in this other universe that you have created for yourself, you must be inspired by reality, for example, by going to administrations such as the Chamber of Commerce or Crafts, restaurants, evenings organized by the municipality, inspire and immerse yourself in places and people.

Your thoughts will be flooded with well-being and confidence, the small whirlwind will grow and the big one will shrink, everything should be rebalanced in your life, and this tendency to optimism should increase gradually and according to people.

DO NOT FORCE EVENTS!

Never wait for charity events to happen and let them come to you, the spirit of impatience blocks the good vibrations, if something has to happen in your life, it will happen, always welcome what happens to you with kindness and lesson, learning is never a punishment, learn from this.

Somewhere in Time

A film released in the 1980s with Christopher Reeves and Jane Seymour as the main actors, the story tells the adventures of a man who wanted to go back in time to meet a woman who lived in another era, whose portrait is hanging in his hotel room.

He tried to find a way to go back in time and join the young woman, became an obsession for him and took all the information about time travel, met an old hotel employee who told him "the secret", to travel back in time, he must be immersed in the times until the end, in the behaviors he will have to adopt and in the clothes he will have to wear, and above all, he will have to convince himself that he really is part of the past, and will not have a shred of thoughts referring to his original time.

I'm not going to tell the whole story of the film, but if you're interested, I invite you to see it, it will inspire you.

As in the film, it's not that I encourage you to go back in time no matter how hard you try (you never know), you have to have successful thoughts in mind, keep them alive, and the law of attraction will work in your direction. Don't force things, act as if you already have them and don't expect them to arrive immediately in an instant, the time for the energies to be optimal also depends on the work that is done in you.

Even if your thoughts of success are weak, care for them like the seeds you sow! They will grow and give beautiful plants.

Sometimes it is not enough to change life with very little, and as it is written in the Bible "if our faith is as big as a mustard seed, everything is possible" (Gospel according to St. Luke).

Fifth exercise

Write a positive thought one day like Emile Coué.

Take a blank piece of paper and write this phrase "everything is fine!" "remember what you noticed before putting it in a corner where you can pick it up later. For a week, say it when you wake up "everything is fine", then remember that short phrase during the day, try to calm yourself by saying it yourself. Self-suggesting to yourself

The following week, you will resume your sheet, then add below the first sentence "everything will be fine", the same principle that the first time, in the morning and during your day, repeat this sentence to yourself, whispering it while you continue your activity.

Then, play the same pattern for the same period of time, but adding your first name, as if you were addressing this message.

"you can do it," "you can do it," "you'll succeed."

When you have at least twenty of them, you will get a series of phrases built like these:

"Everything's fine."
"Everything will be all right"
"Yoann, everything will be all right"

"Yoann, everything's gonna be fine, you can do it."
"Yoann, it's going to be okay, you can do it, you can do it."
"Yoann, it's gonna be okay, you can do it, you can do it, you can do it, you're gonna do it......."

It is important to take into account each of these affirmations for the exercise to work, your mind will be impregnated with these affirmations as you gain confidence, you will feel better and better.

Learn them by heart, little by little, week after week, then learn the sequence of affirmations at once, as if you were receiving a twenty-line poem, the repetition auto-suggests to your subconscious, it will resonate in your mind.

Sixth exercise

«Brainstorming»

Write on a blank sheet of paper everything that comes into your head, force your mind, can be anything and everything, unlock your creativity, whether positive or negative things, write everything, your day, your appointments, what is happening now, what happened a month ago.

Then, classify what you've noticed into two categories (positive and negative)

So, for each element of the negative side, find the positive aspects, surely there are some, just look a little. Then report everything in the positive category. Try to convince yourself that you can overcome these events, that you are morally stronger, read your answers again until you are really convinced.

Seventh exercise

It also relies on breathing, and it will also allow you to maintain control of yourself. In a professional or other stressful situation, use this method:

Place the palm of your hand flat, facing up, and place it at navel level.

Breathe slowly through your nose! Gently raise your hand as you inflate your lungs, stop at throat level, and then place the palm of your hand in the other direction.

Exhale slowly and lower your hand at the same time to the belt.

Do it three to five times, at the same time, clear your mind. This should relieve the tension.

Habits to adopt

"Since you can't change the direction of the wind, you have to to learn how to direct the candles."
(James Dean)

Here are the first things you need to improve in order for your positive vortex to grow and for it to reduce the other.

If you really want to change, you have to change your habits, they are not written in stone and therefore can be changed. To transform your external world, you have to change your internal world. A little later, I will give you some techniques that will help you. The perception you will have of it will later be felt in you, and those around you will see a positive difference. In other words, you will be an improved version of yourself.

First of all, rearrange your house so that you feel comfortable, an overly furnished space makes you feel too tight, open the windows and let the light into your house!

Eliminate the habit of leaving everything lying around, on tables, chairs or on the sofa, tidying up the cupboards. Store your papers in folders sorted by subject and date, e.g. bank, rent, electricity, telephone.

Your home is where you spend most of your time, so you'd better feel comfortable there. A tidy home is a sign of a more coherent mind, you put it in order.

When you return home after a long workday, you will notice a state of well-being at home. It is also important for family members or friends who come to visit you, they will see you with a new eye.

You must take care of your environment because it determines who you are. It includes your relationships with others, the places you frequent, the television programs you watch, and your living space.
Go to bed early, don't be absorbed by movies on TV or other distractions, even to read, don't read too late, your body needs to regenerate.

If you have an alarm clock, set it well in advance by setting a reminder and, above all, don't put it next to you! The reflex is that you'll turn it off by telling yourself "a few more minutes and I'll get up! "These few minutes sometimes turn into half an hour or more. Keep it away from you and program it strong enough, it will encourage you to get up.

Every morning, say to yourself this phrase: "Every day, I move a little further toward my success! "No matter what the outcome of this day is, keep in mind that there is always something positive behind the negative, don't remain frozen by these destructive thoughts, create new rituals, new little things that can improve your daily life. Forget the past and change! Forget the future and live the present moment!

If you don't know what to do with your days, make a schedule and put in activities such as 1 hour of reading, 1 hour of job search, set goals and stick to them. Go to the companies, if the answers are negative, try to find out why, ask them for advice and then improve these points. Never concentrate on refusals, take lessons, it will make you evolve. Stop being that overconfident person, you won't get anywhere else. Life is a perpetual learning experience.

Improve your image

Depending on how you dress or behave, others will judge you or believe they are judging you, you will feel complex and uncomfortable in your skin, and of course, this will also be seen on your face.

When it comes to behavior, don't look for conflicts or respond to them! Violence attracts violence and brings no good. On the contrary, if you don't respond to conflict situations, some will think you are weak, but in reality you are strong because you have control over yourself, many don't have the ability to respect others.

Indifference is your best weapon. Also, stop complaining that this or that person," he said, "in talking about you, gives them the satisfaction of greatness when you feel crushed by them, you ignore them, you don't give them the importance they don't have, some are very happy with your misfortune when you respond to it.

Never trust your problems too much, keep them to yourself and act to overcome challenges, never doubt your ability to climb mountains, climbing is hard, but the satisfaction is great once you reach the top.

You must be calm, smiling (not forced), kind, helpful, impassive to criticism and your image towards others will improve.

These are new habits that require strict self-discipline, to do things like "violence", like getting up early in the morning, to which must be added Emile Coué's method of taking a cord of twenty knots, and by pinching each of them, pronouncing very clearly "every day, from all points of view, I am improving more and more", saying it with conviction, chasing away the superfluous, not thinking about your day, just saying this phrase twenty times, Emile Coué recommends to doing it in the morning and at night.

Then, include new habits in your daily life. Make a list if necessary, learn to be kind to people by saying with a smile, hello, goodbye, thank you, these simple words will make you a respectful person.

Be more interested in positive thinking and read a lot, it is beneficial for you.

Cultural enrichment

Also, you can read, if you're not used to it, then there's a beginning to everything.

In your reading it is not necessary to know everything by heart, it must be above all a hobby, and if you are interested in a topic, it will come naturally, perhaps even give you some ideas for your future, because you can be in harmony with the topic or topics.

These new habits will be integrated into your whirlwind of positive energy and will grow and the second representing the negative will diminish. Reading, unconsciously, will bring you the inspiration you lack, your brain is impregnated with it, because it records in spite of everything that attracts your attention. Let your imagination work, it will be your best ally and will give you clues about your future, trust it!

Then you will be less complex, and also, to acquire more technical knowledge, why don't you read books on science, politics or general culture? You will gain confidence in yourself and in your dialogues between friends and professionals.

If you can, do crossword puzzles or sudoku grids to stimulate your brain, it will make you think.

Watching cultural programs on the Discovery Channel or National Geographic will enrich our knowledge, and stopping watching TV series about death and violence will obscure the mind.

It's not easy, you might say, and yet, with practice, we can do it, conditioning our brains, which have become routine for certain thought forms.

Dedicate a little of your time to activities is possible, don't tell me that in 24 hours of time, it's impossible for you, give yourself an hour of time to read, if you're not used to it (I wasn't used to it, by the way!), you'll see that it will do you good.

CHAPTER 5: HAVING POSITIVE THOUGHTS AND REBUILDING HIMSELF

"To reach the truth, we must once in a lifetime undo all the opinions we have received, and rebuild the whole system of our knowledge again. »
(René Descartes)

Turning the negative into the positive, our weaknesses into strengths It took me a long time to understand this, why I wasted so much time drawing my strength from my weaknesses. You have to cultivate a discipline to correct yourself, because I understood that who really can help me is above myself.

To support my comments, let me tell you a little about my story. Like you, I have lived sad moments, but also happy moments, in everything I have lived, I have been able to find inner strength, this implies looking back and relativizing situations, if I had not lived certain events in my life, I would not be where I am today, in these lines of this book.

In my life, and in almost all situations, consciously or unconsciously, I have been able to find an inner strength that has allowed me to move forward, and with time I have realized the usefulness of past events, life puts us to the test, let us be worthy of it.

Don't look at your past, except to get the positive out of it, guilt for past mistakes is useless, sinking us into repentance, what is done, is done, but don't worry! Because things can change right now, I'll help you!

That's what life has taught me, to get up, like when you fall off a bicycle, to be able to ride again and to gain confidence.

Basically, we all look alike from birth, we are neither good nor bad, only we all have an experience that has led us to where we are, to what our parents and associates have taught us by poisoning our minds from an early age.

We have met many people, people who have supported us, others who have been belittled, there have been moments of joy and anger, our feelings have always oscillated, which makes us the person we are now.

Keep in mind that not everything was as bad as it seems, if we had not met some people, we would not have learned those feelings that are, jealousy, motivation, tolerance, or love.

As for the people who criticize you or crush you, thank them, because they have given you an inner strength, which has not yet been exploited, and which I have already used, that force that pushes you forward, that drives you and gives you energy, that force is to fight, not hitting you, but using your head.

When it comes to jealousy, there are people who envy you, believe it or not, and will do anything to destabilize you looking for your weaknesses. Learn to be impassive, knowing where it comes from, it should not affect you in any way.

You need to think about yourself and your success.

To be responsible is not to blame others or vice versa, it is to be aware of your own mistakes and try to remedy them, assume your actions with full knowledge of the causes, even this toxic being that has you under its control, which puts a sword of Damocles above your head. Please don't feel guilty for them anymore.

You're responsible for yourself, just like these people. Life is a long learning process, there are challenges that are necessary to make us even stronger.

To put a picture in my words, when you were in school (or high school), did you copy your classmates?

By having this kind of behavior, learning nothing by yourself and reproducing everything that other students do, you can "block" yourself during exams. But it's too late, on your desk there's a 20-page high school course that's attached without understanding a word of everything that's written on it. You are solely responsible.

It's true, no one will do it for you, you must be able to take responsibility for the evidence, it's what makes you stronger, what strengthens you for your future.

I offer you something precious and unique in terms of personal development, first, a knowledge based on my own experiences, I had to delve into myself to write these lines, to inspire me every day in real life, of course, I studied many books on the subject, I had to understand myself to understand others.

People are just what you want them to be to you, that is, the perception of what you think without trying to understand beyond the real problem, with the risk of scandalizing you, let me ask you a question, and if the real problem was you? Or rather, I would say, your analytical mind, because the brain registers erroneous information from childhood, from your parents if you have not been taught to respect others, and from the friends you have had, who have bombarded your mind with preconceived ideas and have saturated it with bad thoughts so far.

You have been taught what to do and what not to do, to judge others, to respect the elderly.

All the people around you have brought you into their environment, from a very early age you are part of it. They are being dragged into this spiral that is spinning in the wrong direction.

You have had an education with many prohibitions, which is not always bad, but which slows you down in your momentum, having received a bad treatment of the information in your mind.

173

You have been taught to fear poverty and precariousness on a daily basis and you have been given rules for living in society, how to make a living and how to remain dependent. You were intoxicated by the media.

You have been taught to doubt with someone always behind you to show you how to do it in circumstances where you could have learned it for yourself, which created a feeling that you didn't dare to try it for yourself.

Human nature would like an individual to be anchored in the collective paradigm, it is not an organized group at the base, it is their beliefs and attitudes that have been formed by a single person, you have simply done the rest, if you believe that a person is against you, it gives the feeling that everyone is against you. It's in your mind.

There is also the socialization of the environment that gives you habits (good or bad), to do like others, drink, smoke or use drugs.

Like the domino theory, each action leads to another, the mood of others affects you, for example, when someone is angry with you, so you are angry.

An unhealthy climate makes negative thoughts attractive, and they can be read on your face, you blush, you frown, in short, you don't feel well.

I talk about the phenomenon of attraction because negative thoughts act like magnets, their environment affects our mood, our mind captures their waves like a sponge that fills with water. After that, it is not surprising to see what I was talking about before, cyclical with a large spiral of negative energy, and a small spiral of positive energy.

The screams of the children, the arguments, our state of mind, everything around us, calls our attention too much, forcing us to follow the counterclockwise direction, a wrong direction convinced that it is the right one, I would respond FALSE, without really realizing it, you just follow what you have been taught, and it is far from being the right one.

Also, unconsciously, you carry this bad energy with you as soon as you leave your house and meet the people, communicating it to them in turns.

There is a way out of this habit, out of this vicious circle. Cultivating behaviors adapted to positivity and thus creating the right climate to get back on track.

No one is destined to fail, I mean, no one. These are preconceived ideas, you are in no way at the receiving end of a bad spell and it only exists when you believe in it!

The mind is maintained, and a good mood first helps to see life on the right side.

It's all a matter of conviction, everyone is free to validate or not my statements, but in your interest, I advise you to do so.

I have read quite a lot about the subject with different approaches to positive thinking, going through the spiritual and the religious, all my knowledge about the subject returning to the same point, that of attracting good things to oneself.

We attract to ourselves what we send, that is, we reap what we sow, if it is positive that we give, we should expect the positive, if it is negative, we reap the negative, in this sense, the laws of karma are universal, whether giving to something or thinking about something.

Cultivate healthy thoughts in yourself! Erase everything that could be harmful in you, the thoughts you have should not have a negative purpose, that is, if you think you are earning money to impress those around you, it will not work!

On the contrary, if you want to earn money to help others, or for your personal comfort, you want to do it to change your life in another environment, it is more likely to be consistent.

Thinking positive is something you have to work on! It is not enough to think about it, but to immerse yourself in it.

Without going back too far, you have to improve your environment, your friendships, transform all negative situations into positive ones, tell yourself that fortunately you are there with the life you have had.

We must also stop feeling sorry for ourselves and tell ourselves that in our situation, it is not so bad and that we can always recover, nothing is engraved in stone, behind the clouds, there is always the sun.

To help you do this, there are methods, one of which I will give you is a book I read for the first time on the subject, "The Power of Positive Thinking" by Norman Vincent Peal, which deals with self-conviction, how does it work? Think of something very strong as if you already had it. Another is the ability to always keep your mind above the line.

Imagine a line with the negative at the bottom and the positive at the top. Always stay on the top line no matter what.

The notion of "lack"

You have to redirect your thoughts to notions of abundance, look at what you already have and appreciate everything for what it is. Look also at your journey, you are still alive and I hope you are in good health. You have a loving family, people appreciate you for what you are, give them back the same.

As for their desires and desires, they are also synonyms of lack. You need this or that(s), but you don't think you can afford it.

You must have thoughts of "possibility of obtaining," acting as if it were happening, as if the object of your desire were already in your possession.

Imagine yourself in another life, how do you imagine it? Who did you want to be?

The magic is in us

As I said in this book, it is not a magic book, but it has the power to make your subconscious react, which can make your dreams come true.

There is a fabulous power to control thoughts and make them come true.

We can attract to ourselves as much as we want, according to the law of attractiveness. Be careful, there are conditions for it, materialization does not work if your thoughts are accompanied by a feeling of absolute need or to satisfy your ego.

It is essential to think that everything is already within our reach, or that we already have the object of desire, and also, to content ourselves with what is necessary (as Baloo would say in "the book of the jungle"), to be already happy with what we have, if something better has to happen, it will happen without forcing. Do not force external forces to give you what you want, put aside your impatience, your desire is engraved in your subconscious, forget it! And the work of materialization will be carried out.

We always get what we want when we leave behind our desires and hopes, it is a phenomenon called "the last hour", when nothing else prevents the energies from flowing into you.

To imagine what I mean, imagine a hinged door, someone wants to pass by pushing it, but if you also want to pass by pushing it, you block the person behind you, and you don't pass by too. It's as simple as that. Positive energies cannot flow if, on your side, you block access with your eagerness to see things happen.

The balance of energies

One of the lessons to learn also for the realization of our desires is about the harmonization is the gift of itself, the universe must find its balance and each individual who is found is an extension of himself, just like nature.

The weight of a balance must not only weigh one side to obtain the object of your desires, but you must also give something in return, it can be a spiritual or material gift.

The question is "what do you give in return? there are laws, rules to respect, the act must be selfless and not "wait". you have to give with your heart.

It must remain in the karmic spirit of receiving what you give, individuals are extensions of yourself, you must be in the mind of the person to whom you give.

"The "other" is "you" in the quantum mirror, feel his smile when you offer something, it is like giving something to yourself.

Personal anecdotes

One day, I played a game of chance at a tobacco store. At the counter there was an urn to make a donation to a disabled person who wanted to buy an adapted vehicle.

I won 2 € of the 1 € played, the tobacconist wanted me to play again, I refused, I recovered the winnings and put them in the box.

The moral to remember, when we play games of chance, is that if circumstances make us earn a sum of money, as it is, we must receive it with gratitude, and that gratitude must be shared.

With this logic, I have sometimes made large sums of money, and I still share my gratitude for life's events.

We must always offer as if it were us who received this gift.

Here is another personal story that comes to mind, and shows that karma can also work in the opposite direction.

In 2004, I bought a nice minivan for 1000 €. He drove for two years, then one night, in the parking lot of the residence where I lived, an individual cut my four tires.

The car was in the parking lot for a while, then one day I saw a word on the windshield wipers of the minivan, at first I thought it was because the vehicle was on the road, but it was not.

One person in my neighborhood was interested in the minivan, wanted to replace it with a BX or a 405, both being diesel vehicles. The one who offered one of these vehicles was a mechanic, and he took care of it.

I agreed, and shortly thereafter, I went to his garage for a cleaning of the rear clamp, so the technical inspection had not been passed.

With much bitterness he told me that the vehicle he had exchanged with him had problems and that the cylinder head gasket had to be replaced. The van in question, according to him, was worth less than 1000 €.

I had changed for my minivan, a vehicle that served me for at least 5 years without any problem.

The next day I sold my 405, I almost offered it because the buyer had forced me to lower the price a little, the engine let go, while the day before it worked very well.

If there was a moral to this story, it is that bad intentions will always turn against us, it is karmic law, no one can escape it, we are all part of a whole.

Always follow your intuitions

They must come from your five senses, what you see, touch, hear, smell or taste, it is not necessary that all the senses work at the same time, they are references, guides in your life that speak to your heart. Then comes the dilemma between passion or reason, but the latter has its limitations, caused by what you have often been taught and forbidden, the curiosity of your senses has been altered.

I trust very much in your ability to observe, to notice around you those who are successful, to take an example from them, to learn from those who have reached a high level of their lives, to act as if you were them, in terms of gestures and habits, and above all, to try to associate with them to align yourself with their way of thinking.

Watch videos about well-known personalities and imagine being a few meters away. It could be Bill Gates or Steven Spielberg, they are people who have followed your intuition, you will start a discussion with them, knowing their gestures, their words, soak up this.

Then imagine being on their skin and seeing the world with their eyes, how would they see it?

The trinkets

The real magic is in you, it's not found in the trinkets or gray-gray sold in the markets, there's no lucky stone, there's never been a statuette in so-called power, there's never been a miraculous potion (no, but seriously, do you think?) and I would never say it enough, watch out for dream sellers! You would leave your money, your mental health, and I consider these people to be dangerous to you.

Never believe someone who offers to make a lot of money or increase your income with "tips and tricks" that you see on the Internet or anywhere else. Of course they can say it worked for them..........thanks to your money and your ignorance, they certainly get richer.

Gambling and betting

You wonder why you don't win (or rarely) large amounts of money in the lottery or other, the answer is simple, you want to win a large amount, but this is synonymous with lack, a more or less urgent need for money, you make a conscious projection, play with the hope of seeing your wishes come true, while blocking your energies, without letting them enter freely, hence the importance of living in the present moment without worrying about whether you are going to win or not, don't make too many dangerous predictions. Play for fun and maintain a good mood, not to satisfy a lack.

Tell yourself that you have already received this amount of money in your mind and that you are already in your spiritual bank, in the world that you have created for yourself.

"I have learned that courage is not the absence of fear, but the ability to overcome it.
»
(Nelson Mandela)

Tripping for better recovery

If you had the opportunity to see yourself with an external eye, who would you discover? Would you be able to reason with yourself? If the ego remains the same, it will be difficult, you will need an electric shock to change, let life take care of it, and you will understand, it is good advice.

You have to fall off the pedestal to understand that, in the end, we were only a few centimeters from the ground, while you thought you were in a skyscraper.

If life challenges us, we must accept it as a challenge to overcome, your true strength lies in the difficulty and not in the platonic comfort of the fear of failure, you will fall, that is true, but the reward is great when we get up again. One lesson learnt leads to the next.

It's right there, at your fingertips, removes the big block of your doubts and fears. Don't rest on your laurels, do what you have to do!

"Work! Take the trouble! It is the only fund where there is less lack".
(Jean de la Fontaine)

If it is true that all work deserves a salary, the opposite is equally true, one has nothing for nothing, little hope that everything will fall from heaven. Reading my book without making noise on the sofa will not bring you anything without personal investment, it is not a magic book, he only serves to highlight that everything that is already in you, in your subconscious, and gives you references in terms of personal development, you understand this nuance?

The law of attraction requires a lot of personal investment, and the proofs of life must be considered as clues for everything you want, we do not become kings without fighting (even if I had some for inheritance and filiations you would tell me).

There are balances to respect, one must give to receive, not wait for everything to arrive cooked to one. The counterpart is a personal investment, rigorous self-discipline, the ability to be violent and to integrate these habits into one's own circle of life.

CHAPTER 5 : IMPROVING YOUR RELATIONSHIP

"By making our light shine, we offer others the opportunity to do the same. »
(Marianne Williamson)

The solution is in you

It's hard to believe that it's said that way, and yet since you were a child, you've thrown the source of your problems to others, when in fact, a big part of the problem is you, and recognizing it is already a step toward success.

I explain that as a child you had had derogatory comments or criticisms, or that despised you, nothing forced you to believe in them or give importance, but your young age made you naive, in a period of growth and thirst for knowledge, you drowned your brain with false informations.

What may seem quite paradoxical is also that all the people we meet in our lives, who have a negative influence on us, have had an education, a distorted flow of information, only project their experiences onto you.

So you understand that, at some point, you are not yourself, you are not shining with your authenticity, but you are unconsciously reproducing everything that people have taught you in your life.

His judgments about particular individuals are altered, so he perceives them as good or bad, depending on what he has been taught. They give you the image that you give them.

For example, when you begin to be kind, you give an image of someone nice and frequent or, in the worst case, you will be seen as naive, on the contrary, if you give an impression of pettiness, insulting everyone, belittling, for some, you pass for a hard man, for others, you are a malicious being.

We are all built in the same mold at birth, we all have different origins, they can be similar or close as well, our vision of the outside world is frustrated, it is difficult to define who lives at their own pace, or who lives at the pace of others.

What unites us and resembles us are our own organic emotions, when our hearts beat wildly when we are in love or excited, or when our nerves flutter when we are angry, giving us all a sense of well-being or discomfort.

The mind knows the difference between the two, but our misconceptions through our culture of life, our teachings, give us the wrong signals.

Personally, I was very well educated, my father and mother were always with me, they were examples. As the son of an Indochinese veteran, I have always cultivated this pride, and I have a mother who taught me fundamental values, respect, dignity and kindness. What has significantly changed my personality is the outside world, another form of culture of life, being bitter, nervous, anxious, the outside world with its noises and violence. What made me who I am.

The biggest job is to do a self-analysis to understand why people are acting a certain way toward you.

Of course, most people judge without knowing, unconsciously, that you are doing the same thing, even if you are convinced otherwise.

Basically, who are you really? We're all used to perceiving ourselves as good or bad, extroverted or introverted, but the signal that defines who you are is the way others look at you.

"Wait for someone to criticize your personality, but don't wait for someone to tell you who you are. »
(Mahamat Haroun)

It is necessary to stop looking at the navel and be interested in others, if you think you are a center of interest and expect people to be interested in you, you are wrong, we are all built in the same mold, and those you find in life are exactly like you, need to be considered, valued.

In a vivid way, when you talk to a friend, you are that friend, with the same expectations, you are not so different from others insofar as you like to be appreciated, how would it be different for them?

Try it, focus your attention on others, and in any case, you will never please everyone, but the majority, which is already good, will make you a disinterested person and will have a good opinion of you. This will change the perception of those around you.

Don't do this while you wait to receive, it must be a free and selfless act, it must come from the heart.

Who are you really, ask yourself this simple question about others, what image do you think you give?

I will propose an exercise based on observation.

Look around and notice the behavior of individuals, of those who observe you, of others in their thoughts, when you observe someone, look at the brightness of their gaze, their joyful or sad look, look angry, listen to the intonation of voices, do not interfere, and operate your five senses.

Analyze without judging, guess their attitudes without any conviction.

Most people spend their time judging when it would be easy to look at themselves, to see who they are in relation to us. You didn't wear their slippers and you don't know what they went through, in fact, you don't know anything.

As for the "we say", don't listen to them too much, ask yourself why they tell you this about this or that person and never let gossip alter your thoughts.

Convictions

Everyone lives with their convictions, those of believing what is right in our opinion, with or without listening to others, and yet it is a serious mistake to live for yourself, it is necessary to learn from them, everything a person tells you about them (leaving aside what some say when they talk about others, you are not even sure if it is true). Learning from others will make you a leader, a selfless person.

Also ask yourself the right questions, when, for example, when, by the way, you "do yourself a favor" to someone, you do it for free, or you do it mostly for your ego, what will it bring you? Recognition, of course, but it will never make you an authentic person.

Do it without waiting for someone to "offer you a medal", it must come first from the heart, if you don't want to, then don't do it.

A good leader acts with his heart, a disinterested attention, the key is here for relational comfort, it is altruism, to offer happiness to others without expecting anything in return, except a great teaching.

Each of us has something to contribute to this world and especially to yourself.

Listen to the joys and sorrows, be interested in being interesting and not in "doing what interests you".

I recommend Dale Carnegie's book How to Make Friends, which will teach you how to improve your relationships at work, with friends and family.

PART III: IMPLEMENTATION

CHAPTER 6: ANALYZING YOUR PROJECTS

"Never give up because you never know what the tide will bring the next day. »
(Tom Hanks)

In professional life

Without knowing everyone's situation, whether you are with or without work, I will try to adapt this section for everyone, because this book is for everyone.

For those who have work, are you happy with your work? And are relationships with colleagues good? Think about these questions and take stock of your professional activity. When you arrive, you have a feeling of moral heaviness and little enthusiasm to come to work.

You arrive a little early to have your coffee and you start quickly, always looking at your watch or the watch behind you, so you take your work with a lot of bitterness, your motivation to come to work is only to have enough to pay your bills, you feel trapped.

In perspective, what has been the case for me is that, on top of that, their bills are paid thanks to their work. This gives your mind some free time to change direction. Isn't that wonderful?

Your salary gives you access to leisure activities, reading, learning, physical or spiritual activities, the key is to take advantage of this security situation to keep your mind free.

Being in a professional situation offers opportunities to get out of the system, some make the mistake of staying in this comfortable situation when their life could be very different, bringing you the maximum.

If you feel uncomfortable in your work, it is because it is simply not right for you, look for another path, go to what is implacably aspiring for you, follow your intuitions, let your heart guide you and always try to achieve it, do not slow down, success is full of traps to see if you are up to it, and unconsciously, you are.

For the unemployed, the answer is simple, is that they have not yet found their way because they lack the means to move, experience or diplomas. You are offered jobs that you tend to reject, because it is not your field.

And yet, if you are offered a job, even if you don't like it, you are not locked in a cage, there is always a way out, I would advise you to take it for a while to turn around, the time to train and be informed.

Personal Anecdote

In the year 2000, I worked at BOUVERAT INDUSTRIE in Marnaz, Haute-Savoie, I wanted to go back to school, I experienced many failures but time was on my side, I took advantage of my situation to inform myself at the Centre d'Informations et d'Orientations about the possibilities of resuming studies.

The woman in front of me was very kind and attentive, she gave me the procedure to follow to return to secondary school and thus pass my Professional Baccalaureate in Accounting through a path called the recurrent session, I was four years behind my future classmates, in the background, I did not see much of this gap, being fixed on my goal.

What saved me was my determination, the rejection of destiny and my beliefs in success, of having taken the time to work, to work on many books, and also, for a period of time, to have followed a distance course at the French School of Accounting.

Spiritual anchorage

When the life plan is elaborated, it is necessary to forge certain habits, sometimes violent, because your state of mind will make you surrender, remember, I mentioned to you that it is absolutely necessary to keep positive thoughts within your reach and to act as if this were already acquired.

Anchor yourself in a project without postponing or wanting to get involved, stay on course!

Christophe Collomb, before discovering San Salvador, had to cross rough seas, looking at the horizon, had a goal and believed in it very strongly, which was not the case of his crew, very restless and frightened, took the navigator by a madman, but Christophe remained impassive and determined, the promised land, what he thought was India, was his destiny.

Be inspired by many of the characters in the story, who have advanced through their strength of conviction, and have never surrendered to adversity.

In the Bible it is written that we must remain on the road, not depart from it, neither to the left nor to the right of its path, despite the mountains, the rocks, the shifting sands, we must have faith.

The important thing is not the journey, but the destination, keep your eyes fixed on the horizon and someday you will see your promised land far away. Your travel companions, your conviction, your inner strength and your serenity.

If I can give you some advice on the subject, do not listen to anyone who destabilizes you, as has been said before, there will always be someone to criticize you, even when you have triumphed in your life, it is almost certain, because we all have an ego, you, me, or others, everyone wants the first place, but there is only one place, when a person is not successful in their projects, he envies those who arrive there, it is inevitable.

Especially in the worst cases, where many people thought you couldn't do it, those who have diminished you, criticized you, seen that you are successful, while they themselves can't, or don't try. But what can we say in the end? It only involves you to succeed, it is you, your future is in your hands, never be afraid to move forward because of others, otherwise you will regret at the end of your life, and by then it will be too late.

Focus on your goals and, above all, document and read a lot. Reading books on topics you like and documentary programs can help you do that.

"It's human nature to be wrong, persevering in error is a vice."

The mistake, strictly speaking, is to believe that we do nothing, to believe that perfection is not of this world is the principle of wisdom, we must love its imperfections, recognize them to improve.

Perfection has subtle aspects, it is to adhere to its qualities, but also to its defects, especially towards others

CHAPTER 7: TAKING THE STEP AND DARING

"In life, we don't do what we want, but we are responsible for what we are. »
(Jean-Paul Sartre)

A young man wanted to be a pilot, despite his dreams, nothing happened, there were no signs of fate, what changed his destiny was that he went to learn about flight courses, fares, even took books on aviation.

He put all the conditions on his side, even visiting the airfields, and it was there so often that a mechanic working in one of them noticed it and wondered what he was doing here.

The young man told him everything, and that he was very passionate about aviation, but that he couldn't afford flying lessons because he didn't have a job.

The mechanic thought for a moment and suggested that he return the next day at five o'clock.

Our character spent the night without a wink of an eye because he was so anxious, not knowing what he was going to eat, that he was afraid of missing the date.

He met the mechanic the day before, but what he was offered was not acrobatic training, but to clean up his workshop, he promised to do it every day.

A few weeks later, the mechanic decided to take him on as an apprentice and offered to teach him everything he needed to know about airplanes.

One day, he was surprised to find under a dusty canvas a device in poor condition, it was a Cessna 150L, missing many parts, including propellers and components of the dashboard.

He saw the mechanic and asked why it was stored in the back of the workshop.

The latter replied that he wanted to get rid of it, the young man asked if he could try to repair it, the mechanic replied "if you want, but outside your working hours".

He spent several nights trying to repair the Cessna, cleaning it, it still lacked many parts, including some parts of the engine.

He worked hard and passionately, bought the missing parts, fine-tuned the adjustments, months passed and finally, the plane was ready to take off, there were still some formalities before that.

What happened next will surprise you, he auctioned his aircraft, the sale took place and he raised a very good amount of money, and with what he earned, he bought his pilot's license. He started a pilot's job for a private individual, leaving him part of the money from the sale, and set it aside until he could pay for his own plane.

Do you see? With determination, motivation, passion, we get to everything, we just have to put a little of our own, meet all the conditions for everything to become a reality, the young man vibrated so enthusiastically that he was noticed by a mechanic, was the starting point of his success.

What about you? What's his starting point? Do what he does! Hold on to your dreams, put your heart into them and everything will come true, don't sit like a goldfish in an aquarium, act now and learn to accept failures as your allies, as an opportunity to make it better, you will be guided to success when you have exorcised the demon of "everything succeeds at all costs"!

Start today even if you haven't finished this book! You roll over and start over, it's essential! But above all, don't give up! It is when we stumble upon a rock that we see the rock.

Pick up the phone, if it can be used for anything other than trinkets, there may be someone to contribute to your success, behind the line, it's like behind the mountain, beyond the horizon, it's always that sweet unknown behind the doubt and fear.

The more you jump into the water, the more confident you will be of yourself. Don't take your mistakes for granted anymore, do the same thing again, but with lessons.

In February 2012, I left my native Haute-Savoie to try my luck in Rodez in Aveyron, one of my old acquaintances had offered me a job as driver and deliveryman for GLS and TNT, companies specialized in express parcels, located near Olemps, a few kilometers from my place of residence in this department that I only knew by name, I had brought some suitcases in my car. My training was assured for two weeks before throwing me to the Causses, a route of several kilometers between Balsac, Clairvaux, Marsillac Vallon, Saint Cyprien, Conques and Le Grand Vabre, to return to Mouret and to return safely to Rodez. It was intensive, not only was it necessary to follow this training, to handle the packages in the delivery order, to know how to use the sheets and scan them, then to know the department that was not an easy task when I only had my maps and my GPS. You can't imagine the stress it caused me, but with effort and determination, I almost made it, the companies I worked for realized that it took me too long to complete my deliveries, finishing very late at night, sometimes at 10 o'clock at night.

However, I do not regret the experience, which was very enriching, allowed me to meet charming people and beautiful landscapes, the positive point of all this is to have taken the step, I had to dare to venture, towards that unknown that is the domination of your fear, to go beyond my limiting beliefs, because I knew nothing and I did not even know where I was going, as the terrain was unknown to me, far away from the mountains of Haute Savoie. I experienced failure, yes, but I returned to my mountains with fond memories, a department culture I didn't have before, and I knew where the failure was, so I wouldn't do more transportation, which is a sure thing.

The image is quite edifying, but how can I show you what I see? There are mountains around me, and behind me, there is an unknown that is destiny. Be curious, don't just stand there and "contemplate the mountains" (for those who live in flat terrain, it seems less obvious), look at the horizon and see how far it extends, aren't you curious to know what is far? Perhaps your success, or perhaps a failure (I know! Normandy's answer), there is always the possibility of sitting there looking the other way with the beer or soda in hand, but I doubt it will be productive for you.

Daring is breaking down barriers, mountains, or anything else that blocks your path, going beyond your doubts and fears, finally knowing the future of your project, accepting also that we can fail or succeed in life, then you start over on a new basis, you know your mistakes, and therefore you can learn to avoid them.

Get out of your campaign! Don't be afraid of the clash of civilizations when you arrive in the city!

Succeed or fail, but move on!

Sometimes, you have to follow paths that are not directly related to what you want to do, but can take you there, for example, any job allows you to have the money to help you take correspondence courses, it is essential to have social stability first (which is the union minimum to be successful).

For those who knew the former CEO of the Total group, Christophe de Margerie, he really started at the bottom of the scale, as a simple intern. It is because he invested body and soul in this company that he climbed the ladder one by one to reach the top.

There is also another strategy that can be used, the meeting of executives who are directly related to your project, as long as they don't tell you, because they don't like the competition, nor future competitors, and want to keep an exclusivity of what they produce and sell, keep it for themselves and be friendly to them, they will take the opportunity to go fishing in the news. It may sound a bit hypocritical (we live in a world without scruples, don't forget it!), but what you want to do is the best way to do it, leaders are not able to give up their secrets and love "industrial patriotism", they praise the company they appreciate, and like the fable of the crow and the fox, they will open their wide beak, but I doubt there will be a cheese, rather beautiful opportunities, take them!

What Many Employers Will Not Tell You

I'm going to tell you a secret about employers, when you read a job offer, you see that you don't have the required skills, and yet it may be "you" what the company is looking for.

An employer often needs someone who is persistent and dynamic beyond the technical or conventional aspect. Being this person involved in the company because it requires a personal investment, not especially diplomas or experience (which are an advantage).

Be thirsty for knowledge and don't be afraid to ask employers questions, this shows that you are interested in them. Do not come to them with an arrogant look and giving the impression of knowing everything, especially if you know more than they do, have their pride, do not try to overcome them, they are the ones who will lead you to surpass yourself.

Cut the rope behind you

If you tend to want to return to the bridge of success, leave the bridge behind you, you have no choice but to move on, pick up the phone and know how they say: "in the fait accompli, contact companies right now or training centers to get information and, when something interests you, commit yourself fully. Meeting people, even if you don't find what you have to say interesting (basically, what do you know about it?), what matters is first contact, talking. It is useless to limit ourselves to a few organizations or people who can help you, see more broadly, the possibilities are many. Don't back down again, otherwise, all your life, you won't do anything more than that. TAKE MEASURES!!!!! FURIA!!!!!

The search for false excuses

If you want to achieve what you want, you have to really invest in what you do. Sometimes we give up when it costs us too much, when we don't have time, money or few technical resources, in short, there is always an excuse for everything and that delays us.

For example, for silver, if you believe that all those who succeeded were born under the same star, with a golden spoon in their mouth or a silver tray placed in front of the cradle, you are already wrong. For example, celebrities who haven't started from scratch and have enjoyed dazzling success, such as Renaud, Florent Pagny or Soprano, or politicians who don't belong to the National School of Administration (ENA) either.

You believe that success is due solely to luck, it would mean that you were born in another world, those I mentioned have worked hard to get where they are. He was talking about Florent Pagny, whom I consider a compatriot, because he left his native Haute-Savoie to go to Paris with a goal in mind, to get into music, with great audacity and determination, he did it.

You also have a project that is close to your heart, go ahead, try it, try it, try it, don't get stuck in fear and excuses.

Time, we can find it, there are 24 hours in a day, don't pretend you don't have time, sometimes you find it to play video games or to watch television on uninformative subjects, I doubt very much that Dylan's divorce from Wendy in *The Young and the Restless* will give you the solution. It's even more profitable to devote 1 to 2 hours a day to your project if it's really important to us. Stay true to your dreams, don't give up anything, even if your environment doesn't encourage you to do so, I repeat, it's your life and everything that will result from it.

Personal investment is essential to the law of attraction, having positive thoughts is good, and it is even better to adopt the precepts on a daily basis.

In my life, from a very early age, I have done many projects, some have been successful, others have failed, I have never stopped advancing, studying new strategics, curious about everything, the last one is to write a book, even if the conditions have not been too favorable. Imagine living in a climate where there is a lot of noise, the neighbours chatting on their terrace, the young people screaming, the television making noise in the apartment next door. And on top of that, at the beginning of the lines of this book, my hand got stuck on a door, and it hurts a lot to type on the keyboard. Do you think I'm limiting myself to my project? No!

The mass of concentration that I must have had, and also the inspiration that this situation gives me now, to be able to use it to my advantage, what gives me so much strength and determination is to try everything in my life, without giving up for one little fool or another.

Previously, in my youth, I went to school on foot or by bicycle, sometimes in heavy rain. What motivated me was to tell myself that I was almost there, and make another effort. A few more meters and I was already there. I have also lived this situation in my professional life, the whims of time have not stopped me. Exhausted by the long walks, I immediately set to work.

During my national service, during my maneuvers in Valdahon in 1999, I walked 15 kilometers under the snow and with a t-shirt, I soaked from head to toe, I carried my backpack that pulled me from the back, the strap of my Famas grazed my shoulder and warmed my skin. When I arrived at the barracks, I was soaked like a soup, my first idea was to find a towel to dry myself, I still didn't realize the effort I had made.

Compared to our elders, they travelled dozens of kilometres to the coal mine, in a very old age when there were no cars or bicycles, the most privileged only had the plough. Many of them slept in the place, and spent the week or even months without seeing their loved ones. When you meet the oil rig workers and they stay there without getting to land when they want to.

What those who triumph and those who fail share is determination, the will to achieve it, and there are no excuses to hide.

Tell yourself this, you have nothing for nothing, when you cannot find a job in your field, do something else in the meantime. If you do nothing, the situation may get worse, employers may label you as inactive because you have been out of work for too long. Imagine their faces when they see your resume, look at you with doubt, and ask the fateful question, "What have you been doing all this time? »

If you could imagine the jobs I have to do, you wouldn't believe me. I've been in many fields of activity that could be "people's villages" on my own, in turn, I've been an industrial worker, sweeper, garbage collector, counter salesman   in distribution..
....

.... Rarely have I been inactive, of course, there have been periods of unemployment like almost everyone else, but that is no excuse not to look for anything, to stay at home and wait for it to happen.

If the job they offer you doesn't suit you, take it, if only so that you can afford to study in the field you want. Your work will finance your studies. And if I had personally placed myself in a particular position, I certainly wouldn't have gotten my degree, I wouldn't even have taken a training course at the Chamber of Commerce and Industry.

So, to make sure the attraction is at its maximum potential, live in the present moment! Work, study your project! In any case, "do it! It's very simple. No dangerous prognosis, no excuse, what will happen will happen, but if your thoughts and actions are in adequacy with the attraction, anything can happen, especially the best.

When you can't pull a parallel bar, do two, if you can't do two, do three, if everything seems impossible, do everything possible, it's up to you to succeed.

218

A few years ago, a man tried the unthinkable, swimming through the Channel. He had no arms or legs and yet he succeeded, despite his disability, his name was Phillipe Croizon (look on the Internet). If an individual is capable of achieving the impossible, why not you? Everything happens in the head, you have to have a strong mind.

You have the choice to remain in reverie and apology or to move on, "it's depend of you to see!". "(Régis Laspalès).

The story of the beggar

In the middle of a pedestrian street, on a Saturday morning, a young man sat down in front of a closed shop and asked passers-by for money. Perhaps he was only 20 years old, with narrow shoulders and worn shoes. His clothes have certainly seen better days, and so has he. Frozen in his sitting posture, his shoulders leaned toward the floor.

In front of him, on the tar, a small cup and a piece of cardboard that was partly in his hand and which reads: "I am blind, help me, please". In the cup, there were some coins. Not much.

Then a man approached. He was wearing a well-made suit jacket, cut from an elegant black fabric. Above the black trousers, he wore a white shirt with an open collar and leather shoes. When he reached the beggar, he stopped, reached into his pocket and threw some coins into the cup.

He pretended to leave again, but stopped again, suddenly. With a sudden inspiration, he turned to the young beggar and took the piece of cardboard in his hands. After a brief examination, he quickly made up his mind and began writing on the other side of the poster. Then he placed it again in front of the young man, so that the side he had marked would be visible, wished him a good day and continued on his way. Astonished and thoughtful, the young beggar listened to the man's footsteps as he slowly walked away.

Shortly after, something changed: the cup filled faster than usual. The young blind man could not believe that people had suddenly become more generous. He wondered what the former stranger might have written in his sign to create this effect. He got the answer when a little later the man came back in front of him. When he heard the voice of the man saluting him, the beggar recognized him and called him. He asked the stranger what he had written on his cardboard. His reply astonished him: "Only the truth. I put on exactly the same as you, but in other words. His sign says, "Today is a wonderful day and I can't see it.

As you will have understood, there is no point in stumbling if your strategy doesn't work, ask yourself the right questions, analyse the possibilities of achieving your objectives.

Role-playing games

"It's by doing anything that you become anyone."
(Rémy Gaillard)

Of course, it is not necessary to do anything in this chapter, the book on the subject is very serious, and at the same time entertaining.

Do you know all the role-playing games that involve putting yourself in a character's shoes? They look like costume dances (without the fantasy), the purpose of the experience is to be a kind of chameleon, becoming the man or woman you always wanted to be.

To do this, you will need several elements, including knowledge about the field you want to practice, I recommend that you read books on topics that interest you to learn and that you have a minimum of theoretical knowledge (very important).

The advantage of reading several books on the same subject is that you have different visions and approaches that can be assimilated, that some do not necessarily understand for others at first. There is a phase of consolidation and deepening, as I have already said, do violence on this part, set the daily goal of reading 25 pages, it is better to start slowly, do not skip the steps, this can demoralize you. You can also watch documentaries on the Internet and on television.

Little by little, it will become part of your daily routine, once you have assimilated many of the elements, we can move on to the second part.

To be taken seriously, you have to be careful with the choice of your clothes, what you wear will give your interlocutor a good or bad impression. What to avoid are jeans with holes, faded t-shirts and dirty slippers. Do you honestly believe that an employer will welcome you in this outfit? He'll interpret it as a lack of seriousness and respect for him in three quarters of the cases, so be very careful how you dress!

My suggestions? City shoes, a small shirt or polo shirt, very clean black pants or jeans, closely shaved and well groomed.

You can also choose a suit, but be careful with the colors, I recommend that you stay within the standards if you do not want to look eccentric.

If you're not used to it, wear a white shirt and an anthracite (or black) suit, black shoes without spots, no tie, unless you want to be a seller, and in perfumes, wear something discreet, ask the seller of perfumery some suggestions, she is there to inform you.

Look at yourself in the mirror! You are beautiful, another version of yourself, difficult to recognize your other self. That suits you very well, who is this handsome young man or this beautiful young woman?

Your body must be straight, I propose an exercise that I do every day personally, move your shoulders back and keep your head straight, it will give you a better posture, and repeat in yourself "yes! I am proud of what I have become! »

The look, you must have it on the face of your interlocutor without giving the impression that he is staring at you, look at his eyes from time to time without insisting, this could destabilize the person in front of you. You must have a global vision of the person in front of you.

Active listening, a technique learned during one of my ENL (Neurolinguistic Environment for the Uninitiated) courses.

It is about being attentive to the person in front of you, analyzing each word, using your imagination to live with him everything he says. Begin your sentence with "if I understand correctly" and listen to and include the end of your speech for the following parts

Example :

"If I understood correctly, you have a very interesting offer for CDs."

He answers you a long time

You answer at the end of what he mentioned. "A promotion on such a date?"

He still answers you again.

You tell him:
"In this shop?"

And so on.

However, don't do it too often without including a question about the subject you are dealing with, otherwise you will feel that you are making fun of him or her.

Include questions after repeating the end of your sentence, so that he or she will see that you are interested in him or her.

Now you have a good posture, but you also have to work on your speech, so I keep recommending that you read many books, get informed and talk to serious people who are usually found in administrations such as town halls, during commemorative ceremonies, or in shops specializing in selling sofas (you will observe their sales techniques), in beauty salons or at exhibitions. There are even coaching seminars adapted to your needs.

It is important to know how to speak well, to work on your speech, it is difficult to design someone in a suit that talks like the local market fishmonger, learn to speak quietly, prepare your sentences in your head and structure your answers.

This is the draft of the "other version of yourself", the best you have.

To get back to the part I want to deal with, as you will have understood, there is first and foremost a preparatory phase, a change of appearance so that it changes the way others look at you and others.

Now, what about implementation?

You can try this (do it seriously), practice in front of a mirror beforehand.

Make an appointment with a bank that doesn't know you, and preferably away from an area where you are known.

When you arrive for an interview with a counselor, tell him or her that you have investments to make and that you come for informational purposes (I'm pretty sure he or she will try to have you as a client after what you tell them).

You tell him that you have the sum of 100,000 euros, although at heart you know that this is not true, and you ask him for advice on how to invest in stone and on interest rates.

From then on, you will make a simulation, you will look at the expression of your face, be careful, you will probably ask questions about this sum, you will answer that it comes from an inheritance and that you were surprised to have such a sum.

On a personal level, I have already had this experience for a sounding institute in Toulouse, it was very enriching, the impression of being another person.

CHAPTER 8: SOLUTIONS THAT CAN HELP YOU MOVE FORWARD

You've finally reached this last chapter, congratulations! Turn around and look back and see how far we've come! Impressive, isn't it?

You see exactly what you're capable of, and what you thought was insurmountable isn't insurmountable.

I've taught you the basic principles to get everything you want in your life, but it also requires a personal investment, so I've challenged you.

Don't be afraid, it's easier than it looks, everyone who knows can do it. But you also have to be aware that the theory is good, but putting it into practice is better, you will come out stronger from these experiences.

Coaching

Before this book, I told you about the notion of helping others, but what about getting help?

We live in a world where it is difficult to do without others, even for a company that needs subcontractors and customers to operate in perfect interaction. Your employer needs you as much as you need him; he offers you a job to do for money.

In some circumstances, we are all complementary. Imagine that! Even a head of state always has communication advisors and ministers for the day-to-day management of the country, these same ministers have advisors and secretaries, all these little people working in harmony.

Will he be able to run a business if he doesn't live up to the expectations of customers? Assuming what they want without asking them? We always need others in all circumstances, even in their current situation and unconsciously! They need advice and information, even training.
You can't know everything, there's no infuse science, we all have defects and we must accept them, but we can compensate for some of them through reading and learning, but you and I won't have a universal knowledge of the world. Only God has this power. To recognize it is already to be intelligent.

To return to NLP training, if you want to participate, you can go to the Information and Orientation Centre, which is not far from your home, or to the Chamber of Commerce and Industry near your place of residence.

Build a network that will form your collective brain, insists Napoleon Hill on this point in his book titled "think and get rich".

A few years ago, I saw a film entitled "The Invincible", which tells the story of two teenagers, one paraplegic and the other unable to understand mathematics, each with a quality that the other did not have, made an alliance and managed to overcome the challenges through their complementarity.

A doctor does not do accounting, or at least is not an expert in this field, must turn to a management professional, who cannot make a medical diagnosis or issue a prescription. If you find your own area of expertise, they will never do everything and you will need to seek outside help.

Even I, who write a book, need a proofreader, an editor and other professionals, we are not "one-man band".

"If you want to go fast, go alone, if you want to go far, do it together. »
(African proverb)

Alone, we are isolated, it would be absurd to try an adventure alone, without support, without a client or supplier. All personalities will tell you that we all need a coach or family to support us.

You can find support in various ways, you can come from books, videos, talk to colleagues or in meetings, if you are looking hard, everything is at your disposal.

CONCLUSION

We are coming to the end of this book, hoping that I have given you all the necessary answers to what you expect of it. For those of you who were not used to reading, you may have found the time to read it for a long time. For the author, it is even more so, having to reread it several times during its creation to make sure that nothing is missing, it is in its quite complete sense, I hope wholeheartedly for you.

Do as he does, read this book as many times as necessary, absorb all the advice I have given you, and everything should now go the best way to success, if you have been diligent, it will be guaranteed.

If I can give you some recommendations, and it will serve you all your life, even after your success, being in the field and not talking about your projects with those around you, find the right people to answer the questions you are asking yourself. Live the present moment, act in the direction of your projects without seeking success, because it will come without forcing. Maintain a positive mind, be it curious, and good surprises will await you in the end, I guarantee it.

Returning to the beginning of my book, the "secret" that one person told me on New Year's Day at the Chamonix casino, I hid many clues on the subject, for those who doubted it, this meeting really took place.

By the way, I'm going to reveal a part of the message that was written on the paper, this is what he said: "....There is no opportune moment to start a new life, the moment to act has always been present! The action is still there and makes us what we are...... !»

What you have to understand from this short message is that even now, you are in action, I am writing these lines, and you are reading them. It is very important to understand what you have now and what you do with it afterwards, what direction to give to your inspirations, to do your best without expecting a good result, but always fighting for what we believe is right and good for us and our environment. Never stop believing, never think about failures and learn from them, that is the great secret of success, believing in your ideas and giving them a body.

Time is very valuable, don't waste it on trivialities and fantasies, don't look at the train of life without being a passenger, you will always stay on the platform waiting for the next one, but how long will it take before it arrives? Will you take it or wait for the next one? Our existence has a more or less long horizon, and whatever the duration of yours, make the rest of your life the best it can be.

As for those who have criticized you, judged you, despised you and probably still do, you say that these people who are toxic, you will see them stay on the platform through the window of your train, when it leaves, you will see small dots in the distance behind you, you will be comfortably seated in your seat, all this why? Because you decided to do it.

I have put in your mind the seed of success, it is up to you to keep it.

With these last words, I sincerely hope that you can put your projects into practice.

With a cordial greeting

Yoann MERITZA

BOOK SUGGESTIONS

UN MONDE DIFFERENT

— MAXIMUM SUCCESS
Max PICCININI

— UNLIMITED TRUST
Franck NICOLAS

— THE LAW OF ATTRACTION
Michael J. LOSIER

EDITIONS BELIVEAU

— 7 ESSENTIAL INGREDIENTS TO DOMINATE THE LAW OF ATTRACTION
Jack CANFIELD – Mark Victor HANSEN – Jeanna GABELLINI – Eva GREGORY

POCHE MARABOUT

— LA METHODE COUÉ
Emile COUE

— THE POWER OF POSITIVE THINKING
Norman Vincent PEAL

J'AI LU

— THE SECRET CODE OF YOUR DESTINY
James HILMAN

— FULFILL YOUR DESTINY
Wayne W. DYER

— WHENEVER WE WANT, WE CAN!
Normann Vincent PEAL

— HOW TO MAKE YOUR LIFE A SUCCESS?
Dr Josephe MURPHY

— HOW TO USE THE POWER OF YOUR SUBCONSCIOUS MIND?
Dr Joseph MURPHY

— THE POWER OF THE WILL
Paul-Clément JAGOT

— THE GAME OF LIFE
Florence Scovel SHINN

— YOUR WORD IS A MAGIC WAND.
Florence Scovel SHINN

— THINK AND GROW RICH
Napoléon HILL

— THE SECRETS OF COMMUNICATION
Richard BANDLER & John GRINDER

— BECOME A MENTALIST
Bastien BRICOUT

LE LIVRE DE POCHE

— HOW TO MAKE FRIENDS
Dale CARNEGIE

— HOW TO SPEAK IN PUBLIC
Dale CARNEGIE

EDITIONS ASKA

— SMARTER THAN THE DEVIL
Napoléon HILL

EDITIONS ADA

— THE SECRETS OF SUCCESS
Sandra Anne TAYLOR

EDITIONS BUSSIERE

— THE SECRET DOOR TO SUCCESS
Florence Scovel SHINN